# READY, SET,
# Read and Write

Marlene Barron

with
Karen Romano Young

A Skylight Press Book

John Wiley & Sons, Inc.
New York • Chichester • Brisbane • Toronto • Singapore

To my grandchildren, Sarah, Alexander, and Benjamin

—M.B.

For Bethany

—K.R.Y.

Illustrations by Elaine Yabroudy

This text is printed on acid-free paper.

Copyright © 1995 by Marlene Barron and Skylight Press
Illustrations copyright © 1995 by Skylight Press

Published by John Wiley & Sons, Inc.

The publisher and the author have made every reasonable effort
to ensure that the experiments and activities in the book are safe when
conducted as instructed but assume no responsibility for any damage
caused or sustained while performing the experiments or activities in this
book. Parents, guardians, and/or teachers should supervise young readers
who undertake the experiments and activities in this book.

ISBN 0-471-10283-0

Printed in the United States of America

10 9 8 7 6 5 4 3 2 1

# Contents

# Introduction

I f you want to help your child see reading and writing as natural tools of communication (like listening and talking) and sources of enjoyment, growth, and sharing (like eating and playing), you've come to the right place. This book is written for parents of children of about ages three through seven. It's designed to help you make the most of these vital years when your child moves from babyhood to childhood, from your lap to formal education, from seeing letters as black marks on a page to understanding them as words and producing them as his own form of communication.*

Some of you may already have a child in school and are looking for ways to foster a love of and a facility with reading and writing. In this book, you'll find activities that work in tandem with your school's approach and that make reading and writing part of daily life at home.

Some of you may have a younger child. You'll find ways to use the daily events of family life—whatever they may be—to give him the best possible base for using and interpreting written language.

What's the best way to enhance your child's life during these years? The creators of many materials on the market today would have parents believe that their children are empty vessels, waiting to be filled up with information and skills they "need" to move forward in a linear fashion.

Nothing could be further from the truth. In this society, children live amid printed words as never before. Children are predisposed, by nature and by their motivation to make sense of the world around them, to try to make meaning of the letters, words, symbols, phrases, names, and sentences that swim before their eyes each day. No matter what your child's age, he already knows a great many things about language, and is ready to build on that knowledge to become as expert at reading and writing as he is at walking and talking.

As head of a Montessori school in New York City and a longtime specialist in early childhood education, I've seen children learn to read and write in a number of ways. The ones who

* I'll use *he* and *she, his* and *her* interchangeably until the English language evolves a word that means both.

1

experience the most success and who carry a love of reading and writing into adult life are those whose early years were spent using language—talk, reading, and writing—for their own purposes and in their own ways.

This book will show you ways to encourage your child to use language through work and play—any day, in any situation. I have gathered and developed these fun, challenging activities during a quarter of a century of teaching and observing the growth of young children, so I know that they work—and that you and your child will enjoy doing them.

While the book gives you step-by-step instructions for each activity, the activities are open-ended. This means that you can make them your own: use them as starting points, change them as you go along, and end up with a different outcome each time. Through these activities you can create the kind of environment that gives your child plenty of opportunities to learn. Unlike many of the other books designed to prepare children for school, this one does not have lists of required skills, facts, or field trips without which your child will not "measure up." Rather, I'll show you games to use with your three-year-old that will still be a hit when she's six. I'll show you ways to use books, toys, the TV, the sandbox, the grocery store, the computer, and even the refrigerator door to guide your child into exploring new uses of language. And I'll show you how to look at your child *today* so that you see what she already knows about writing.

Each activity is designed to help you give your child experience in a specific area of reading and/or writing. Everything you need is here: a list of materials, step-by-step instructions, and an explanation of the activity's purpose. Built into each activity are ideas for developing the activity further as your child moves along, for extending it into other areas, and for using it with more than one child.

I'm willing to bet that many of these activities will help you become more involved with your child and more confident of your child's natural abilities and talents. You might not use every activity. You might not use any of the activities more than once. Try what appeals to you. Make changes to suit your needs and your child's needs. Make the activities your own. The goal is to make reading and writing a beloved, easy, and comfortable process for you and your child to share together.

## The Educational Philosophy behind the Activities

Here are some of the general ideas that you'll find throughout the activities.

### Whole Language

My preferred approach to the process of learning to communicate is called *whole language*. It incorporates all the ways we use language to make meaning *of* the world and *in* the world. Meaning-making happens every time spoken or written language is interpreted or created, at whatever level and in whatever form it occurs: as conversation, dramatic play, scribbles, drawings, scrawled letters, printing, cursive, computer print-outs and typeset print; on the phone, in the sand, on the sidewalk, in a letter, in junk mail, on a cereal box, in a science book. Whole-language learning takes place everywhere—in the bathroom, kitchen, car, mall, subway. It is not about teaching specific skills or trying to instill skills or concepts in your child one by one. It's an all-day, whole-family experience that can't be stuffed into a workbook or an hour of time.

Language learning is a social process, learned by people, through people. When I say *language* I don't mean just words; language includes visual representations and nonverbal languages.

Children as learners absorb the *sounds* of language, its *meaning* (what words, phrases, and sentences tell us), and its *grammar* (the syntax of the language or how words fit together to create meaning). When you hear words spoken, you receive a whole impression that encompasses the actual words that are said, when they're said, why they're said, and how they're said. You know a lot more than you would if you took in those various pieces of information separately. For example, "Hi, Sweetie" conveys a different meaning when said by a grandma to her grandchild than when said by a passing stranger to an adult.

Written language, too, is as much about the medium as it is about the message. Readers learn to get behind the words to the context—who's saying them and why—by reading a great variety of materials, studying the pictures that go with them, and talking about them with others. When you make reading and writing a part of your child's everyday life, you're helping your child learn these skills as naturally as he learned to listen and talk.

So, how do you get your child involved in whole-language learning? She already is. As a baby begins talking because she's surrounded by talk, a child begins reading and writing because she's surrounded with books, letters—print of all kinds—and paper and pencils. She grows to understand that people around her get meaning from these printed or hand-written words. They see lists, reports, stories, letters, each of which has its own meaning, purpose, and response. If your child is exposed to many uses of writing and many experiences with reading, it's natural that she'll work to develop this tool for communication just as she developed speech.

Just as a child's babbling is progress toward talking, a child's attempt to hold a book while babbling is progress toward reading, and a child's scribbling is progress toward writing. Whole language is about the whole experience of language, not just the end products of reading and writing. This book offers you the information you need to see your child's progress and to support your child as she moves from spoken and heard communication to the understanding and production of written language.

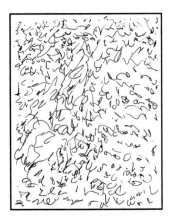

*Scribbles.*
—Jackie Bach,
3 years 10 months

Note that many of the activities in this book overlap with other subject areas. Clearly a child who writes about her trip to the park will cover what are typically thought of as science, math, or social studies ideas. In schools they call this "Reading (or Writing) in Content Areas." I like to call it using language in our whole life. After all, language is used to understand the world, to make sense of the world, to express ideas about the world—the *whole* world!

*Translation Unknown.*
—Jackie Bach, 4 years old

### Understanding Processes

When children go to the YMCA to learn swimming, they are placed in classes based on their ability and their enthusiasm for the water. There's a clear continuum at the Y: "Eels" can jump in, get their heads wet, and dog-paddle to the side. "Minnows" can jump in the deep end (over their heads!) and swim freestyle, more or less, to the other end. "Flying Fish" are ready to learn strokes that require skill and strength; they can even dive. Kids who learn to swim over a number of years at the Y know where they've been and can predict where they're going. It's a far cry from saying "I can't swim" or "I can swim." They've got it broken down into steps: learning to swim is a process, and everyone engaged in that process is said to be "swimming."

The same is true of reading and writing. There's a natural progression from talking to someone to writing to him, from playing out ideas dramatically to drawing them, from drawing stories to telling or writing them. As children grow in listening, talking, reading, and writing, they go through a process. In order for you as a parent to understand and appreciate your child's ability to swim, to talk, to climb, to read and write, it helps to understand the process she goes through to reach those goals. It helps the child to be able to see the process, too.

Children in my school don't learn to say, "I can't read" or "I can *really* read;" rather they learn to say, "I read like a three-year-old" or "I read the pictures." Encourage your child to make these kinds of statements—and to know what they mean—and you give her the same power and confidence those Y swimmers have. When you help children to see that there's a process in just about everything, they learn patience and confidence in their own ability to solve problems and move ahead to the next step.

The understanding of process not only helps a child to be gentle with herself and to appreciate her efforts to read and write, it also helps her to accept her mistakes (and those of others), to set realistic goals for herself, and, most of all, to enjoy *where she is right now*. Research shows a correlation between a child's willingness to take risks (and make mistakes) and the ability to read and write. The children most willing to take risks are those who understand process, who thus see that

*Marlene, we need more Kapla blocks to make a giraffe.*
—Sophie Sakellariadis,
4 years 11 months

a mistake is something you learn from, that most everything could use some fine-tuning, revising, or straightening up. The activities in this book stress process for that very reason. It's vital, also, to put a name on the process itself: "You're reading!" or "You're writing!" At the Y, everybody swims. In your house, everybody reads and writes.

Many of the activities in this book involve children in everyday activities that are processes—doing laundry, washing dishes, shopping for groceries. Each process has a beginning, a middle, and an end. The more processes your child sees, the better will be her approach to any task, including the big job of learning to read and write. Start with Activity 7: Take This Job and Chart It or Activity 8: Talk Me Through It for specific guidelines for involving children in processes.

Once, I was reading with my grandchildren. Sarah, age six, read aloud from a favorite book that she knew by heart. Then it was four-year-old Alex's turn. He picked up *Rosie's Walk* and looked over at Sarah and me. "Hmp!" he said with pride. "Sarah reads the words. *I* read the pictures. That's what four-year-olds do." Now, that's what I call a well-educated child. He knows that he reads and writes as a four-year-old does, not as a six-year-old, a thirty-four-year-old, or even his fifty-five-year-old Bubby does.

### Skills and Concepts

While much of the educational material on the market focuses on building specific skills, this book will instead help your child develop an understanding of needed concepts.

A *skill* is an activity that can be learned and that can improve with practice; for example, cutting with scissors, riding a tricycle, or printing your name. A *concept*, on the other hand, is something that can't be taught directly. It's something each and every person comes to understand on his or her own. A very young child thinks that an adult is reading him the pictures in a book. As he grows, he realizes that the black markings below or beside the pictures are the key to the words. That's a concept: that those symbols (what we call print) stand for a story. Sure, you can *tell* him, but until he realizes that the symbols you see are going into your head and coming out through your mouth as words because you *understand* their intent, he won't really *get* the concept. Eventually he'll grasp that concept through experience, as he watches and hears you read. He'll absorb other concepts, too: that a group of letters makes a word, that letters represent sounds, that words in a book do not change with the reader. A child learns by observing and doing. He takes the information in, ponders it, and makes hypotheses. Eventually he comes up with a concept.

This is not to say that children won't or shouldn't acquire skills through activities. Take Activity 26: Rhymin' Around, which involves taking turns finding rhymes that may be just sounds at first, then nonsense words, then real words. First, children pick up the concept of a rhyme: a word that ends in the same sound. Soon enough they'll find words in their own vocabularies that rhyme, that are real words. As they read (with you at first) books of poetry or nursery rhymes, they'll come to realize that words that rhyme often end in the same letters. That leads them to an understanding of the sounds those letters make. Sure, it might seem faster to teach the sounds the letters make. But would it be the same? Would your child understand as naturally and as enjoyably? Would there be room for trial and error, nonsense and reality, me and you?

Every experience provided through the activities in this book will help your child to develop concepts that will lead to a skilled understanding of written language and a happy confidence in using it.

## About the Activities

The activities in this book are chock-full of my philosophy of learning. They will help you create literacy experiences out of just about any situation, in and out of your home. They encompass games, chores, work, and play. The activities are organized into the following areas:

**Part One:** **Creating the Right Atmosphere.** These activities involve using materials and daily activities to create opportunities for your child to explore written language.

**Part Two:** **Mainly Reading.** These activities help foster enjoyment and proficiency in reading.

**Part Three:** **The Writing Connection.** Here you'll find many ideas for bringing writing into your child's life.

**Part Four:** **Language Ins and Outs.** These games and activities will help your child make connections between language, movement, household doings, and so on.

You don't have to pursue the activities in order. Jump around. Pick and choose. Generally, it's best to choose what appeals to you and to your child's interests, doing activities from each section, picking out what fits in with things you do already. Then change, adapt, and mold the activity to make it your own.

For each activity, you'll see the following structure:

- **Name of Activity:** the title, followed by a few words telling what the activity is about, what its heart is.
- **Helps Develop:** concepts and skills addressed
- **Before You Begin:** actions to take and things to consider before starting
- **You'll Need:** a list of materials
- **What to Do:** step-by-step directions
- **Follow-up Activities:** ways to redo and build on the activity in the future
- **What's Happening:** an explanation of what your child stands to gain from the activity as well as how it relates to school experience
- **Moving Ahead:** ways to take the activity to a higher level
- **Helpful Hint:** a word of advice or a reference to a helpful book or material

Each activity is labeled with the places where you're most likely to use the activities: around the house, out and about (market, mall, library, pool), close to home (yard, garden, park, street, woods), and from here to there (in transit, public or private).

## How You Can Get the Most Out of the Activities

### Understand Your Child's Development

Here are some things that really scare parents: watching other people's children, hearing what teachers say about children, thinking about what they themselves were like as children, and fearing that somehow things are not as they should be with their children. *Relax!* I've shared the information I'm about to share with you with many parents over the years, and I've never seen it fail to bring a smile of relief.

Children change rapidly. Your child today will be different from your child yesterday. But you worry, Is she growing fast enough, far enough, soon enough? Some educators will attempt to answer that question, and may even place your child on a chart to show you where she is in terms of development, and how she compares with other kids. This is hogwash! It's impossible as well as unnecessary and unhelpful to pinpoint a child's position scientifically.

● ● ● ● ● ● ● ● ● ● ● ● ● ● ●
*Donna can I bring the crickets home on our vacation.*
—Sam de Toledo

Kids develop at different rates physically. Look at all the shapes and sizes of your child's playmates. Well, rates of emotional, social, and intellectual development are as diverse as rates of physical development. Celebrate how interesting your child's development is rather than worry about it. "How?" you ask. Here are a few basic tips:

- **Don't push.** When your previously independent child climbs into your lap, don't worry. Hug that kid. Don't protest, inwardly or outwardly. Instead, give that child what he's asking for, to fill up on. Cuddle kids until *they* don't want to hug *you* anymore.

- **Don't compare.** "Comparisons are odious," said a poet. They are not needed in formal education, and certainly not in the kind of informal education that is the premise of this book.

- **Don't be overly concerned about testing.** Some schools will tell you that they use tests to determine something called "mental age," as opposed to physical or chronological age. The score is often based on a brief interview that a total stranger has with your child, some questions, and an assessment that places your child on a continuum with others of the same chronological age. Research has really *not* documented the validity of such testing for predicting future "success" in school. No test can judge a child's motivation to learn, enthusiasm about school, ability to reason and solve problems in a variety of situations. These kinds of tests are based on comparisons among children. They judge a child on a specific day, in an artificial setting, and using questions that are often meaningless for the child. Even worse, such testing has been shown to influence how parents and teachers treat a child. This can ultimately harm the child's self-esteem.

### Accept Your Child's Developmental Level and Interests

"She's writing, all right," one mother told me. "Sentences and sentences of invented writing. But she doesn't use very many letters. They're mostly *E, M, I, L,* and *Y.* And the dog's name is in every sentence. When she reads to me, her name and the dog's name aren't even part of the story."

"Perfect!" I said. "That's where she is."

This child was using letters she knew to express herself, and was reading them as what she wanted to express.

That mother came to me feeling negative but left feeling positive. If you can accept that your child is on the road to somewhere, at a step in the process of learning, you won't have to worry that she's going nowhere. Above all, be interested and receptive every time your child wants to share reading and writing activities with you. Practice and experience will lead her on.

### Acknowledge Your Child's Abilities

If acceptance is about attitude, acknowledgment is about words. In general, make statements that affirm your child's place in the reading and writing process and encourage your child to state her position in a similar fashion. Say you have a four-year-old and a six-year-old in the same family. The last thing that four-year-old needs is her big brother saying, "You're not reading. You're just looking at the pictures." The four-year-old needs confidence to reply, "Four-year-olds read pictures. Six-year-olds read words."

Or suppose your child sits at the table with his crayon and paper, saying, "How do I spell *dog?*" Since the notion of "correct" spelling will keep him from writing fluently, your answer might be, "I write *dog* the way grown-ups do. You write it your own four-year-old way." Don't be concerned about spelling.

He'll grow in spelling as he grows in other writing mechanics. More importantly, you'll see plenty of writing from a child who's not afraid to express himself—in pictures, scribbles, letters, words, and finally, sentences—because he's been accepted all along for what he's doing.

However, you don't have to be completely inflexible in this. One problem that arises in many homes is that the child knows the adult can't read her invented writing. She knows that one of the most important purposes of writing (besides self-expression) is communication. She wants to communicate, but she writes like a four-year-old. Encourage her to write anyway. Then she can translate her work for you as you write it in adult writing. Explain, if you like, that even adults don't speak or write all languages.

● ● ● ● ● ● ● ● ● ● ● ● ● ●

*Dear Susanne, You can come to our class breakfast. Signed 4E.*
—Katie Starer, 5 years 3 months, and Alex Harvey, 6 years 8 months

### Help Your Child Develop Her Senses and Physical Strength for Reading and Writing

In general, information about the world is perceived through the senses and then interpreted into language. The senses are physical, and so, naturally, physical problems can cause sensory problems, which, in turn, interrupt or delay development of language skills.

The abilities to write and speak are also physical. These tasks are easier for a child who has had plenty of experience with using tools (all kinds, not just writing tools) and whose mouth muscles are toned and exercised. Articulation also seems to be affected by diet—not necessarily the nutritional value, but the texture. Poor articulation—"mushy mouth"—may result from just eating food like macaroni, American cheese, and peanut butter. Be sure your child eats the equivalent of "an apple a day." Something else to watch for: hearing loss resulting from minor upper respiratory colds or infections that fill the tubes in the ears with mucus. If a child has a lot of runny noses, she spends a lot of time not hearing clearly. This can affect language development. Keep an eye, also, on a child who has allergies, chronic ear infections, or nasal congestion; he may not be hearing some of the sounds around him. Kids adapt so well that many adults don't notice a problem, but one may be there. In fact, if your child has congestion or ear infections, pay close attention to his language development, and if you or his teacher have a concern, see a specialist.

### Boost Your Child's Confidence

Who's in charge? When it comes to your child's work, the answer, of course, is your child. Approach any work—drawing or writing or whatever—as if you were an editor meeting an author or artist. You're trying to help her express her ideas as clearly as possible, to create as fully as possible, and to feel comfortable and joyful in the process. Here are some encouraging phrases:

"I see a lot of red here. What were you trying to do?"

"What a colorful drawing. Would you share the story with me?"

"That story really gave me the shivers."

"I loved hearing you tell me about watching the foxes at the zoo with Mom. How can we save that story?"

"Thanks for reading that story to me. What a lot of hard work it took to write that!"

Notice that you're not commenting on the use of letters, or judging whether something "really looks like" what it's meant to be, or offering your own interpretation of a story or drawing. You're letting the child interpret his work for you, and drawing on that to make your comments. Your goal is to act as a supportive coach or a mentor.

### Share Books

Read everything and talk about it. Interrupt your reading to ask a question or to answer your child's question. What does the book make you think about? What else do you want to learn? How does what you read make you feel? Share your intellectual and emotional responses with your child. Exclaim, muse, laugh, giggle, wonder, cry, be sad. Use such phrases as: "That was scary!" "The thing that interests me most . . ." "I liked the part when . . ." "I was so surprised that . . ." Ask your child what her favorite parts were or how the book (or chapter) made her feel. Talk about your shared or perhaps different feelings and ideas.

Also talk about other stories or information the book brings to mind. Read other books about a topic to check out different angles. Read several versions of a story. *Cinderella*, for instance, has many versions, including those from other cultures: the Perrault version that's most popular in our culture, the Disney version, and odd adaptations like *Cinderella Penguin or the Glass Flipper*.

Why is it so important to talk about books? When children *hear* language (either oral language or book language), they become familiar with the pattern of the language, the sentence structure, the intonation, and the vocabulary. What's more, *talking about* a book offers an opportunity to wonder about the author's intention. As in any good conversation, the participants—the adult and the child—are figuring out a meaning together. "I wonder what's going to happen to . . ." "I didn't expect the . . ." "What's a chocolate sandwich cookie?" "That's funny!"

Most of all, reflecting on and talking about a book brings it closer to home, makes it a part of your day, makes it a part of your conversation, a part of your relationship with your child.

### Explore, Explain, Discuss

Learn the art of the rhetorical question. "I wonder . . .?" "What if . . .?" "How . . .?"

Asking open-ended questions (questions that start with *why* or *how, what if* or *what do you think about* rather than questions that are answered with *yes* or *no*) requires you to become less of an expert. Open-ended questions require your child to become more of an explorer.

Each activity in this book can be introduced through a rhetorical question. The key action is to use an everyday situation, ask an "I wonder . . ." question, and open it to the child to find out or to figure out. I'm certainly not into scripting interactions, but here are a few examples:

"I wonder how many different ways to print *A* there are in the signs on this road?"

"Look at this huge pile of socks. I wonder how we can find all the pairs."

"Gee, what do you think Curious George would do if he were here?"

Listen to your child. Look at your child. Watch what he does. And watch your language: none of this is a test. It's a game.

It's an adventure. It's a way to find out what your child knows—and he knows such a lot! It's a way of opening up new possibilities, new learning opportunities together. In other words, you can't find out whether a child understands how to match colors, textures, and sizes by asking him. Children can always *do* more than they can *explain*. You've got to get together with your child, toss the socks on the bed, and start matching them up.

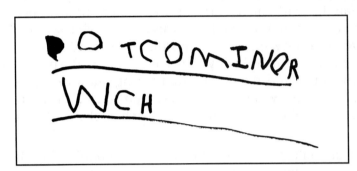

. . . . . . . . . . . . . .
*Don't come in or watch.*
—Jeremy Cohen, 5 years
4 months

Talk through the processes you follow every day, explaining how you do what you do and why you do it that way. Without this experience, children just see the end product and think, "You're perfect. You decide to do something and you do it, magically." That's how it can appear. Most of our everyday processing is invisible to children. Speak aloud about what you're planning, thinking, doing. "See, I'm looking through this coupon circular. I'm thinking about whether we buy any of these things. I'll cut out the ones for things we buy—here, why don't you do this one. Then, we can take the coupons to the store, and they'll give us back money when we buy these things."

Encourage your child to talk about her explorations and experiments. If she's arranging shoes, first involve her by simply doing it yourself while talking aloud. "Let's see. I could put the shoes in a line, or I could . . ." Another time, invite the child to do the job. Later, comment on her arrangement. "I see! You put them together from smallest to largest." Another time: "I'm going to try to figure out how you did this. Hmm. An interesting pattern. Boots, boots, boots, sneakers, sneakers, sneakers, slippers . . ." or, "A mish-mash pattern. Hmm. One of mine, one of yours, one of Dad's . . ." And don't forget to acknowledge your child's accomplishment: "You figured out a new way!"

### Getting Your Child Started with Reading and Writing

So you want to get your child started? If your child is already born, then you *have* already started, through the atmosphere you've created in your home. Children learn to read—and to enjoy reading—by seeing people around them reading and writing. It doesn't so much matter *what* is being read, as long as your child sees people enjoying and using the experience of reading and writing. In fact, a mix of reading materials is preferable. The reading matter can range from *People* magazine to *Pride and Prejudice*. The writing your child sees can include checks, notes, and letters. This atmosphere is what I call a literacy stew. The best stews are the ones that take a long time, that start in the morning with a bone and some water and simmer all day, with new ingredients added as the day goes by: herbs, wine, vegetables. What I wish for all children is that they might grow up sloshing around in a literacy stew in their homes.

You can create a literacy stew for your child out of all the reading materials and writing materials you have around the house. Here are just a few of the "ingredients" your child will benefit from: newspapers, letters, bills, dictionaries, magazines, novels, catalogues, comic books, television, food packages, picture books, and posters. Let him see you reading. Tell him what you're reading and why you're reading it. Read it with him.

Also let your child see you write reports, grocery lists, letters, notes, checks, stories, charts, calendar reminders, journals, and more. Talk with your child about your reading and writing. And make tools of the writing trade available to your child: pencils, paper, crayons, notebooks, pens, erasers, pencil sharpeners, envelopes of various sizes, a typewriter, a computer, anything to write with. Also folders, portfolios, scrapbooks, albums, magnet letters, building blocks with letters, rubber stamps, stick-on letters, rub-on letters, and so on.

Show her how to safely use things like pencil sharpeners and rubber stamps so she can work independently. Share your knowledge of how to use written language to communicate by inviting her to join you. Surround your child with reading and writing, allowing her to see the full extent to which the written word is part of your life.

For more specifics, turn to the activities in Part One, Creating the Right Atmosphere. These activities run the gamut from household tasks to watching television and are designed to help you see various aspects of home life as opportunities for learning to read and write.

This literacy stew—like any good stew—doesn't require a major financial investment. Sure, you could go to a children's bookstore and buy the place out, but this is unnecessary and expensive. Do make a point of choosing quality literature at all levels. Also, provide an *assortment* of contemporary stories, folk tales, joke books, nonfiction informational books, how-to books, puzzles, plays, magazines, picture books, and stories. Such a smorgasbord shows your child the ways the written word is used in our society.

Here are some guidelines for choosing reading materials for you and your child:

- Choose materials that appeal to *both* you and your child. You're going to read them together over and over. Your child will pick up on your feelings toward books you read.

- Look for picture books in which the pictures enhance the story rather than just illustrate it. The best picture books are those in which pictures and text work together to tell the story.

- Some of the most popular children's stories are didactic and unimaginative. Aim for stories that expand your child's horizons, rather than filling your shelves with familiar characters, cute images, and trite plots.

- Note that award-winners are not always the best reads. Judge for yourself. If you do need help, rather than relying on book awards, ask a librarian for a list of good books for young children.

- Consider a subscription to a book club or a quality children's magazine like *Ladybug* or *Crayola Kids*.

- Buy paperbacks. They're cheaper than hardcovers, so you can buy more. Books are meant to be used, not displayed or stored out of reach. Very expensive books are often treated like good china—not used enough.

- Provide nonfiction as well as fiction. Provide chapter books and storybooks as well as picture books. A child of three will listen—and gain from listening—to a short story told well.

- Share and trade books with friends.

- Use your public library to the hilt! Librarians are extremely knowledgeable. Take advantage of their collections, programs, and advice. Borrow, borrow, borrow!

## A Final Word

I was rereading *Bread and Jam for Frances* for the umpteenth time to my granddaughter Sarah. We had read several pages together when Sarah asked, "What's jam?"

After I got over my shock, I asked, "You never ate jam?"

"No," she replied. So I explained, comparing jam to jelly. As she unfurled her brow, she said, "Start the book again, Grandma!"

I knew just what she meant. How different every British novel I had ever read became to me when I first visited England. I wanted to go back and reread them all, because now I understood the context. I had experienced an English summer, sat in an English garden, and eaten typical pub food.

One of the biggest challenges to all readers is context. When anyone, adult or child, gains an understanding of something—an "Aha!"—everything else around it also has to be reunderstood. Give your child all the experiences you can with language, and you give him plenty of chances to say "Aha!" Give your child the opportunity to ask his "What's jam?" questions, and you provide him with the support he needs to move ahead.

One of the biggest challenges to all writers is mechanics. Children have such great ideas. They act things out, they dramatize their scenarios, but when they write their stories, just four lines come out. Why? Because writing involves using a tool, a pencil or keyboard. Because it involves concepts: capital letters, punctuation, the connection between letters and sounds. Understand how complicated this can be for your child as he writes.

Your child will learn to read and write in her own way. For me, it's fabulous to watch it happen over and over, with each different child, in so many different ways. The key is to accept what the child's doing, on his level. Nobody says to a child who has spread paint on paper, "That's not a painting. Here, look at

*The female cricket died.*
*The male cricket walked on*
*the ceiling. He does not like*
*strawberries. The male*
*cricket died.*
—Sam de Toledo

Rembrandt. Now that's a painting." Never! That child is on his way to painting.

In the same way, a child who reads with the book upside down or writes with invented writing is on her way to reading and writing. When adults accept a child's work on her level— three-year-old, six-year-old, twelve-year-old, and so on—and focus on the communication that is taking place, then that child grows in confidence, takes more risks, writes more fully. Do this with your child, and her life and yours will be richer for it.

"Write this for me, Mom."

"Read this to me, Dad."

"Listen to this!"

"See what I wrote!"

Strive to create an atmosphere that accepts and responds to each request and effort, and everything else will follow. Your child is bound to give you something to kvell over. (*Kvell:* what an adult does and feels when his or her child does something absolutely wonderful.) It's a moment to celebrate, a moment to know you're parenting really well, when your child has taken a risk, has asked you with every confidence, "Can I read you my story?"

# PART ONE

# Creating the Right Atmosphere

So, you want to create a literacy stew for your child—a rich brew of opportunities for reading and writing. This section covers the ingredients, mostly things you already have and activities you already pursue, and offers new ways to rethink them, set them up, and use them to help your child explore language.

In this section, I'll focus on family life—how to approach doing household projects with your child, choosing what to display on your refrigerator, watching television, using the family computer, and putting toys, books, and other materials to use for the good of your child's growth in reading and writing.

# 1 What's on the Fridge?

**H**elps develop: *child's ability to create a system, evaluate work, draw and write*

*Is what's on your refrigerator door what's in your heart? What does your child think?*

**Before You Begin**

Reevaluate your use of the refrigerator door. Stock up on magnets, and make your fridge over as a family sharing place. Students at my school have a choice about their work: throw it away, give it away, or take it home. But what happens when work arrives home? Do only "A" papers make it to the fridge? Who decides?

**You'll Need**

a refrigerator door; magnets or tape; items to display

**What to Do**

1 Clear the outside of the fridge.

2 Talk to your child about the need for new refrigerator material. "What do you think we ought to use this space for?"

3 Together decide what part of the door should be used for each type of thing you want to post. Where should notes go? Photographs? Artwork?

4 Assign your child a few magnets to use for her own stuff. Tell her she can post whatever she wants on the refrigerator door. Designate magnets for other family members.

5 Hang a few items up. Help your child with hers if needed.

**Follow-up Activities**

- Talk about what each person decides to put on the door. Discuss the display. Ask your child, "Why is this important to you?"

- Talk with your family about how often—and how—your display should be changed.

**What's Happening**     So many things in a household seem to take place around a child. There are systems set up before the child was born or without her input. In some households, for example, the refrigerator door becomes a parent's place for displaying things, including a child's work. This can mean the parent makes a value judgment, deciding which work will be posted. This activity brings your child into this system, putting that decision into her hands and asking for her opinion and ideas about changes.

**Moving Ahead**     Use your space to write notes to family members, to post rules, or to make requests. "It's mud season! Take off shoes at the door!" or "Six days till my birthday" or "Write your name under what you want for dinner: pizza or tacos?"

**Helpful Hint**     Use things you take down as material for a portfolio or family scrapbook. See Activity 3: A Kid's Keepsake.

# 2 Private Journal

**H**elps develop:
expression
through drawing and
writing, reporting on
real life and imaginary
events and ideas

*Jamie showed me her journal one day. On the very
first page, in her own invented writing, she had written,
"Now I am six. I can read. I can write." A journal can
help your child, too, develop pride in writing.*

**Before You Begin**  Make up your mind not to look at your child's journal unless
invited (if you can't do this, go on to another activity), not to
give instructions, and not to remind your child to write.

**You'll Need**  a blank notebook; pens, pencils, markers, crayons; date stamp
and ink pad (optional)

**What to Do**  1 Give your child the notebook. Tell him that this will be his
own personal book, to do with as he pleases.

2 Provide pens, pencils, markers, and crayons.

3 Show your child how to use the date stamp and ink pad to
mark his entries.

4 Leave your child alone to work.

**Follow-up Activity**  Be a willing, nonjudgmental listener if your child wants to read
aloud to you from his journal.

**What's Happening**  Through writing a journal, a child learns to see writing as a
pleasure and an outlet. When you give your child a jour-
nal, you're giving him a vitally important message: "You can
express yourself however you see fit without my assistance or
direction. Whatever you do in this book is for you alone, to use
as you please, to never look at again, or to share with the
world."

But what if your child isn't writing at all? Remember that
drawing and scribbling is writing. Even a young child will be
happy to have his own place to lay pencil to paper.

**Moving Ahead**    Suggest ideas for other journals. How about writing a journal from the viewpoint of the cat? Of a goldfish? Of a tree or a school? Talk together with your child about what such writers would say.

**Helpful Hints**

- Read to your child from your own journal.
- Read to your child from journals such as

  *Three Days on a River in a Red Canoe*
  by Vera B. Williams (Morrow)

  *Only Opal: The Diary of a Young Girl*
  by Barbara Cooney (Viking)

# 3 A Kid's Keepsake

**H**elps develop: interests, sequencing, categorizing, expression through visuals, writing, and use of scissors and paste

*Let your child choose it. Glue it. Peruse it. Review it.*

**Before You Begin**  Find out what your child is interested in collecting: pictures of toys, places, people, or pets; magazine advertisements that appeal to her, letters from people, baseball cards, postcards, and so on. Then, you can form a purpose for collecting: to learn about animals, or to explore things she'd like for her birthday, or to gather favorite family memorabilia. This is an activity that can be begun and finished in an afternoon, or you and your child can add to it over a lifetime.

**You'll Need**  a scrapbook (store-bought or made at home by stapling or sewing heavy paper inside a cardboard cover); magazines, photographs, newspapers, letters, birthday cards, book covers; paper and pencil; crayons; scissors; glue; tape

**What to Do**  
**1** Set out the scrapbook and explain the basic principle: "This is for keeping stuff in. You keep the stuff in the book by gluing it or taping it in."

**2** Talk to your child about what stuff might be collected. Look through magazines and other materials. Come up with a general theme: animals, pink things, or pictures of neat places. Or suggest that your child just start picking out stuff she likes.

**3** Explain how things are cut out and then glued or taped in and give the child the materials necessary to do this.

**4** Leave the organization of the stuff up to your child. Let her take her time choosing and cutting out pictures, sorting through stuff, and categorizing items in her own way.

**Follow-up Activities**

- Talk to her about what she's doing when she has finished gluing a few things in. Discuss her reasons for her choices and organization.
- Encourage your child to continue adding to her scrapbook now and in the future.

**What's Happening**

*You're encouraging your child to make a system out of a chaos of possibilities, an important skill. By sorting through and studying an assortment of objects, a child naturally learns to group, differentiate, and order items in a variety of ways. These skills are highly necessary to becoming a reader who knows the difference between letters, words, and sentences, not to mention storybooks, nonfiction books, and periodicals. What's more, your child is learning to express herself visually, taking a group of objects and arranging them to her own liking, with her own ideas. Eventually she'll be doing that with letters and words.*

**Moving Ahead**

Acknowledge and respond to your child's interest in each item in her scrapbook. Point out real-life items that resemble ones pictured, write letters with her so she'll get more to add to her collection, find postcards and other pictures in shops and magazines.

**Helpful Hint**

Share your child's baby book with her. Talk about the items you chose and the words you wrote to help you remember your child as a baby. If you have the kind of baby book that goes until your child is about eight years old, have your child work with you on creating new additions to the book.

# 4 The Movable Feast

*Just imagine how many letters your child will look at during his lifetime.*

**Before You Begin**  Play around. Let your child explore movable letters, sort them into colors and shapes, try them in different configurations, pile them up. Are letters and words playthings? Sure!

**You'll Need**  more than one set of movable letters: magnet letters, letter tiles, or cards with letters written on them. Be sure to have lots of each letter. It also helps to have a big, smooth surface to work on: a floor, a refrigerator door, a large cutting board, or the back of a game board.

**What to Do**
1 Spread the letters on a smooth surface.
2 Pick out a letter.
3 Follow the shape with your finger. Encourage your child to do the same.
4 Look for and find another letter like your letter.
5 Now ask your child to choose a letter, trace the shape with his fingers, and find one to match it.
6 Keep on until you've matched all the letters.

**Follow-up Activities**
● Compare your child's letter with yours. How are they similar? How are they different?
● Tell your child the names of the letters you chose.
● Make a chart with the letters. That is, put all the *A*s in one line, then all the *B*s. You'll end up with a basic bar graph that shows at a glance what you have the most of.

**What's Happening**    Movable letters help your child in many ways. They acquaint him with the names of letters and their uses, and allow him to move letters around (he's erasing and revising when he does that) easily and without fear of error. When your child plays with letters, he's elbow-deep in the stuff of words, using the same materials that Shakespeare, The New York Times, *and Dr. Seuss do. When your child plays with letters, then moves into using them to write his name and other words, he learns that writing is changeable, that writing is his own. Everyone learns the alphabet, but we all use it in different ways. Let your child's alphabet be a pleasant, fun, safe introduction to the tools of reading and writing.*

**Moving Ahead**    Leave messages for your child with the letters. Wait for him to notice, guide his attention in the direction of the words, and read them to him. This process is just one way of letting your child know that words have important meaning in his life.

**Helpful Hint**    Keep it light. One child who had a set of letter tiles that had been her grandfather's only wanted to sit and sort them into rows of like letters. This was fine: she had created her own system of organization, and she reveled in it.

# 5 From Alpha to Omega

**H**elps develop:
*letter recognition,
initial sounds, reading
left to right, connection
between illustrations
and words*

"A, *you're adorable . . .*"
"A *is for apple*"
"A: *ape in a cape*"

**Before You Begin**  Find a selection of alphabet books in your library to explore with your child. The key here is exploration. Just teaching children the names of the letters does not enhance their ability to learn to read. Kids who know the alphabet song at two don't necessarily become great readers. The deciding factor in most cases is a rich experience in having been read to.

**You'll Need**  alphabet books; a blank book to make your own alphabet book; drawing tools; magazines; scissors; glue

**What to Do**  **1** Read several different alphabet books with your child.

**2** Talk with your child about the similarities and differences between the illustrations and words used in each book. Talk about each author's use of uppercase and lowercase letters.

**3** Ask your child to pick one letter of the alphabet.

**4** Take a few books and open them all to the letter your child chose. Talk about all the different words the books use for that letter. Do the words all start with the same sound? Which words and objects does your child know? If there's an apple tree on the *A* page, for example, talk about whether the apples look like the one your child ate for lunch today. Discuss strange new words and objects with your child. Help her identify them, make guesses about them, and find out more. You might say, "Gee, what's an ibex? I wonder where ibexes live."

| **Follow-up Activity** | Invite your child to make her own alphabet book with a blank book or sheets of paper stapled together. Ask your child to choose one letter to illustrate exclusively, or to do the whole alphabet, as she prefers. Have your child draw illustrations or cut and glue in pictures from magazines, label the pictures with words (or tell you the words to write), and create a cover. Have your child read her book to you or another person. |

| **What's Happening** | *Research shows that children who read alphabet books with their parents receive two kinds of information: information about the uses of graphic form, and information about how people use books. Use alphabet books as a springboard to discussions about capital and lowercase letters, letters in different typefaces or fonts, and differences in the sounds one letter can make.* |

| **Moving Ahead** | Make a study of the alphabet by gathering books, posters, and picture dictionaries to read, discuss, and compare. |

| **Helpful Hint** | Some fun alphabet books to try include: |

- *Anno's Alphabet : An Adventure in Imagination* by Mitsumasa Anno (Harper)
- *On Market Street* by Arnold Lobel (Greenwillow)
- *Brian Wildsmith's ABC* by Brian Wildsmith (Watts)
- *Animal Alphabet* by Bert Kitchen (Dial)
- *Hosie's Alphabet* by Leonard Baskin (Viking)
- *Antler, Bear, Canoe: A Northwoods Alphabet Year* by Betsy Bowen (Joy Street)

# 6 The Daily Mail

*Mail call!*
*Empty the mailbox into your child's arms,*
*and discover a treasure trove for reading.*

**H**elps develop: *purposeful reading, writing, categorizing*

**Before You Begin**  Watch for the mail. Talk about how it gets to your mailbox. Introduce your child to the mail carrier and ask for an explanation of where the mail comes from.

**You'll Need**  a day's mail, including letters, bills, the newspaper, and junk mail

**What to Do**

1 Have your child hold the mail. Talk about it together. Ask questions that identify things: "Did the paper come? Are there any catalogs? I'd love a letter from Aunt Peg . . ."

2 Sort the mail together. Put it into piles by category such as newspapers, magazines, letters, bills, and catalogs.

3 Help your child label each pile with little stick-on notes. For beginning writers, you can write the label. Advanced writers can write the labels themselves.

4 Examine the outside of the mail. Look at the stamps. Read the postmarks: "Look! This took four days to get here!"

5 Let your child open selected envelopes and pull out letters and papers. Read the mail aloud together. Do what you normally do with the mail, but share your thoughts with your child, out loud.

   "Look, bananas are on special this week. Do you think we should buy some? Well, this says we could win a big car. Should we try? Look at these red boots, only $40."

**Follow-up Activity**  Let your child keep the mail you don't need. Provide a box for this purpose. Give her order forms and envelopes, for example, so she can use them for her writing.

**What's Happening**  *The mail is a vital source for connecting each of us with the world through reading and writing. As you sort mail, you show your child the different kinds of writing that exist. When you talk about the mail you receive, you help your child see the purpose of written communication. "I need this bill to see how much we have to pay for electricity this month. We've had the lights on a lot since it's winter. Do you think we'll have to pay more than last month?" or "Here's a letter from the library. We have a book that's overdue." Finally, by having your child write and apply labels to piles of mail, you give her a role in the process of bringing mail into the house, a purpose for writing, and practice with placing things in categories.*

**Moving Ahead**  Encourage your child to use the mail to write and communicate. Help her send away for a cereal toy, write to a pen pal, or mail a postcard. If a toy breaks, help write a letter of complaint. Then wait for a response; watch for the mail carrier!

**Helpful Hint**  Use special, saved mail as material for a scrapbook. See Activity 3: A Kid's Keepsake.

# 7 Take This Job and Chart It!

**H**elps develop:
understanding of
processes, sequencing,
drawing, writing

*Charts will help you say to your child,
"I know you can do this yourself now."*

**Before You Begin**  Think about the things your child can do. Can he brush his teeth? Paint a picture and clean up afterward? Pick a task that your child has practice doing. You'll use this task as the basis for an independence chart, a visual key that your child creates and uses to remind himself of the steps in a process.

**You'll Need**  paper, pencils, crayons or markers

**What to Do**  1  Talk to your child about a task that needs to be done. Talk with him about each step as he does it. "It's time to brush your teeth. What do you need? Toothbrush, cup, towel, stool. What else? Now what do you do?" Demonstrate the steps and the sequence for him if necessary.

2  Then tell him, "I know you can do this yourself next time."

3  Tell your child that you have an idea that will help him remember the steps in the task. Get a sheet of paper and ask your child to help you name each step in order. Draw a picture of each step on the sheet of paper to form a chart. Let your child do the drawings if he wants.

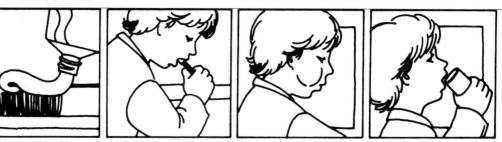

**4** Together, choose a place to post the chart. Discuss which place is most convenient for the task.

**5** Ask your child to use the chart as a reminder as he does the task.

**Follow-up Activity**  Now that your child has had this experience, help him to see it as a tool to remember other tasks. You might suggest, "What about making a chart for feeding the dog?" or "Hmmm. How could you help yourself remember?"

**What's Happening**  *By breaking the job into steps you show your child how it is done—beginning, middle, and end. It's important to choose a process that your child already knows well. The point here is to help your child organize a process into visual steps, while he masters the process itself. Understanding of process—the sequential steps in an action—is vital to your child's development of reading, writing, and indeed all learning. When you give a child an understanding of how a process is done, you add to his confidence and self-esteem.*

**Moving Ahead**  With a young child, use pictures alone to show the actions that are part of each step. Once your child knows that words have meaning, label the pictures.

Allow for revision. Forgot to include the step for putting the cap back on the toothpaste? Talk to your child about where in the process this should go (before brushing or after?), and revise the chart together.

**Helpful Hints**
- Adding machine tape is great for creating horizontal sequences.
- Create charts on a computer that has a drawing function. Help your child to see this as another way of recording an idea. Have him choose or design the pictures to represent each step.

# 8 Talk Me Through It

**H**elps develop: understanding of process, cause and effect, verbal expression

*Your child can be a great assistant, and she'll also learn valuable lessons.*

**Before You Begin**

You've got errands to run, chores to do, work to finish. And there's a small child at your elbow. Take a minute to think of more than one way to involve your child in the job at hand. Here's how to make any activity meaningful for your child.

**You'll Need**

one of your daily activities

**What to Do**

1 Pick something you're going to do today. Talk about it with your child, explaining to her why you're going to do this thing. Tell her the steps involved in the activity. Discuss your choices regarding time, materials, and actions. For example, suppose you need to buy a new storm door. Here are some things you might say:

"I want a wooden door instead of a metal one, because . . ."

"We'll have to look in a few stores and compare prices."

"We'll pick one out and buy it."

"At home we'll have to paint the door first with primer and then with two coats of paint."

"We'll have to figure out how to take the old door off and hang the new one."

2 Now, go do it. Involve your child in all the steps you can by talking to her about what you're thinking, doing, and deciding. "I really liked the one we saw yesterday. Which one did you like better?" Explain your reasoning as you make decisions, keeping it simple.

**3** Give your child jobs that are part of the process. Have her help you measure, hammer, and carry.

**4** Each step of the way, remind your child of what steps came before and what steps come after.

**5** Finish the job, and talk things over with your child. Which part did she find most interesting? How does she feel about the way things turned out?

**Follow-up Activity**   Encourage your child to talk to other people about what you did together, to describe the process, and to be proud of her role in it.

**What's Happening**   You're making your child your apprentice in the chores of everyday life as you explain, demonstrate, and actively involve her. I can't overstate the importance of a child understanding the what and why—the process—of events. What's more, you're giving your child a rich language experience: she'll hear and use new vocabulary, she'll gather information about talking to people in different businesses, and she'll use words with you to discuss it all.

**Moving Ahead**   Ask your child to draw or write about her experience of working with you to meet your goal. By doing this, she'll go over the process in her mind, communicate it, and gain an understanding of reporting and writing about something that really happened.

**Helpful Hint**   Make a list of the steps you need to follow. Talk about the steps aloud, then write them down (or have your child write them). Lists are great tools for understanding!

# 9 The Terrific Tube

**H**elps develop: auditory and visual discrimination, listening to written and oral language, connecting language with real life

*What is the television to you and your child? Garden of entertainment delights? Treasure trove of information? Opium of the masses? Boob tube?*

**Before You Begin**

Set aside an hour to watch TV with your child. Pick a different program every time you do this activity: your favorite show, your child's favorite show, the news, an old movie . . . But don't expect to sit and stare. This is your chance to interpret television for and with your child. Get ready to talk it up.

**You'll Need**

some time to watch television with your child; paper and pencil

**What to Do**

1 Pick a program to watch together. You can do this by studying the television listings and reading the options to your child, or just saying, "There's something I'd like to watch. Want to watch it with me?" Set a time with your child; make a date. Tell your child in advance that you're going to talk a lot about what's happening on the television during this time.

2 Watch the program together. Read any words on the screen to your child. Talk about what the different words mean: titles of shows, credits, advertising words, network logos, telephone numbers, and so on.

3 Sing along with the jingles and encourage your child to join you. Later, you can write down the lyrics of your favorite ones with assistance from your child.

4 Talk about the different ways people speak on television. What's the difference between the way people speak during a conversation and the way they speak during a news broadcast, the weather report, a drama? Prick up your ears

when you hear an interesting accent, language, or dialect, and point it out to your child.

5 Talk about the advertising. Point out that people somewhere have created all these ads in hope of selling their products. Talk about what they're selling. Discuss what they're doing and saying to sell their product.

6 Talk back to the television set. (I do this whether there's a child in the room or not!) Talk about how realistic you think the program is. Interpret for your child as necessary, and open his mind to the possibility that what appears on the tube is not necessarily the truth of the matter.

7 When the program is over, turn the TV off.

**Follow-up Activity**   Talk about what you watched. Would you want to watch that program again?

**What's Happening**   This activity encourages your child to try to understand and evaluate what he sees on television, to talk about what it makes him think and feel, and to turn it on and off according to his evaluations and tastes. Television is an important part of our culture. As a tool of communication it can be a blessing or a curse. By discussing what you see and hear with your child, you help him see this medium as fallible, questionable, acceptable, enjoyable, and rejectable.

**Moving Ahead**   Keep a TV log with your child. In it write a variety of lists: of the things you and your child like and dislike during an hour of television; of advertised items that you'd like to try; of announced shows that you'd like to watch; of characters in a favorite show, and so on. Simply ask your child what he'd like to make a list of each time you watch. This is an easy way of taking new ideas and images and making them your own, of seeing how the words are written, of remembering what you watched.

**Helpful Hint**   Show joy in the things you love to watch on television. Through this you can demonstrate to your child that a well-chosen program can be as beneficial to the viewer as a book, a game, or free play.

# 10 Read to Me

> **H**elps develop: reasons for reading: getting information (nonfiction books), making connections between text and life, becoming part of an imaginary world (fiction books)

*"Richer than I, you will never be:*
*I had a mother who read to me."*

**Before You Begin**

Take a new look at the way you read to your child. Some parents read books five times a day. Some don't read at all. Analyze your attitude toward reading with your child—perhaps you can make reading a more fulfilling experience.

**You'll Need**

a book; a chair; a child

**What to Do**

**1** Say to your child, "How about a story?"

**2** Let your child choose the book from reading material you've already made available to her. Give her the opportunity to explore her books by agreeing to read anything she suggests.

**3** Read. And be dramatic. Use your voice to create moods, interest, and varied characters. Don't worry if you don't feel dramatically creative. Ask your child to imagine how different characters sound.

**4** Stop from time to time, not necessarily just at the end. Let your child interrupt you to ask questions, to start the book over, to read a part again, to study an illustration and discuss it.

**5** Stop if your child loses interest or just wants to stop. Make it plain that this is her book, her time. Don't worry about finishing the book. (Think about how adults read. We don't all finish what we start, or finish a book in one sitting.)

**6** Read the book again if your child asks. Again and again and again.

**Follow-up Activities**

- Talk about how the story makes your child feel. Laugh at the funny parts. Cry at sad parts, too.
- Talk about the words the author uses, the colors the illustrator uses, unusual construction (pop-ups or borders) and typefaces.

**What's Happening**

*Consider two classrooms in which teachers used books in different ways. One teacher arranged and kept her books too carefully. The kids tended to leave them on the shelf. The other teacher allowed books to be left on the floor, steps, and tables. The kids pored over, discussed, chewed on, and read those books. When you read to your child casually, flexibly, and frequently, you make books part of your life, your child's life, your family's life. Make reading as important to your mental health and enjoyment as eating and sleeping are to your physical health and enjoyment, and you'll rear a child who slips into reading as easily as she slips out of bed in the morning. At the same time, by allowing interruptions and alterations, you show your child that books are hers for the taking and using.*

**Moving Ahead**

You're never too old to be read to. Plan on reading aloud to your child—and having her read to you—until she leaves home. One way to implement this plan is to have your child read to you, at her own level, as she grows. Listen, interrupt to discuss, ask for a repeat or explanation.

**Helpful Hint**

It's never too late to start reading aloud. If you haven't read much to your child before, you may encounter some resistance to the idea. Stick with it: "Let's read just one page [or two, or five]. Or let's just look at the cover and imagine what it might be about. We'll stop whenever you want to." And do stop if she asks you to! What's more, start reading everything in sight aloud, as though to yourself: the TV listings, the newspaper, a picture book, a recipe, a letter. You'll be letting your child in on the many uses of reading, and piquing her interest besides.

# 11 Puppet Play

Helps develop: *gross and fine motor skills, understanding of process, dramatic play, oral expression, creating and revising stories*

*Is your child full to the brim with stories?*
*Give him a puppet, and you'll see.*

**Before You Begin**

Ready to make puppets? Talk to your child about the process you'll follow to make the puppets and put them to use.

**You'll Need**

coloring books; crayons; cardboard; tongue depressors *or* popsicle sticks; tape; glue

**What to Do**

1 Have your child select a coloring book and choose several characters (people, animals, or whatever he likes) to make into puppets.

2 Ask your child to color the characters. Since you're going to cut the characters out, he doesn't need to color the background.

3 Glue the colored pages to cardboard.

4 Cut out the characters.

5 Tape a tongue depressor to the back of each character.

6 Use the edge of a table or the back of a chair as a puppet theater.

7 Let your child take the lead in creating a story for these characters to take part in. Ask him what the characters will do. Ask him what roles he wants you to play.

8 Rehearse your parts. Encourage your child to change his story as he wishes.

9 Find someone to be the audience. Use teddy bears if nobody's around.

10 It's show time!

Each new puppet gives your child a chance to try a new voice, a new conversation, a new bit of language. When you work with your child to play with, adapt, change, and create puppet dramas, you help your child see that language can be used in situations he devises. By encouraging your child to think up his own dramas, change them, and perform them, you help him to explore the processes necessary for writing, revising, and publishing stories.

**Moving Ahead**

Anything can be a puppet: your child's drawing of a person, a stuffed animal, a pencil, a pair of underpants (put your arms through and walk around), a salami from the deli (just try it; it's a hilarious puppet), your child's uneaten sandwich. Use any excuse to act out a conversation with your child through puppets.

One father I know spent time waiting in the doctor's office drawing a sick face and a well face on two tongue depressors. The puppets cheered his child up, even through the doctor's examination, and continued to amuse him while he sat getting better on the couch back at home.

**Helpful Hint**

A five-year-old may imagine that a stick is a horse and will let a dog puppet play the role of a wolf. A younger child is more likely to insist that a dog puppet can only be a dog. You may need to keep puppet-making supplies on hand to round out your supply of characters. One toy shop I know carries puppets with Velcro features to put on so that one puppet can be many things. Look for them, or make them yourself.

# 12 It's for You!

*Encourage your child to reach out and touch someone.*

**Before You Begin**  Arrange for your child to get a few telephone calls of her own. Call her to say hello while she's home with a sitter, or have a friend or relative call to say hello. Help your child get accustomed to that vital communication tool, the telephone.

**You'll Need**  telephones: toy phones, old broken phones that can be taken apart and put back together, spare phones, dial and push-button phones, wooden or plastic bananas that you pretend are phones. Have at least two phones on hand.

**What to Do**

1 Stand near a play telephone, looking forlorn. Say, "Gee, I wish someone would call and say hello." Wait.

2 When your child picks up the phone and dials, pick up the other play phone and answer as you would answer your real phone.

3 Be dramatic. Don't look at your child. Act as if you don't know who's calling. Make your caller identify herself.

4 Interrupt the conversation. "Oops! The washing machine is overflowing" or "I've got another call, can I call you back?" Hang up.

5 Call your child back. Invite her to come visit. Make a date.

6 Say goodbye. Hang up.

**Follow-up Activity**  When the phone "rings" again, answer as though you are another person or as though the call is being answered by the phone machine. "Please leave a message at the beep."

A telephone is a tool for conversation, but a conversation takes two. Children often hear just one end of a telephone conversation, and that's no way for them to pick up on the protocol, the clarity of speech, and the other necessary parts of telephone communication.

**Moving Ahead**

*Ring, ring.* A telephone bell means that someone's calling you. A fire engine siren means "Make way!" What other messages do sounds give? Encourage your child to put those messages into words. What's the message of a cricket's call? A car alarm? A honking horn? A dog's bark? The seatbelt buzz in a car?

**Helpful Hints**

- Practice business, social, and emergency calls with your child using play phones.
- Stage conversations in which one or both of you pretends to be someone or something else.
- Practice having your child take phone messages in his own invented writing.

# 13 A Place to Write

*H*elps develop: sorting, value of writing, uses of writing materials

*Virginia Woolf needed a room of her own.*
*Joseph Conrad needed his meals brought to his study door.*
*All your child needs is his own place to write,*
*filled with the stuff he needs to write with.*

**Before You Begin**
Check with your local school system for desks being discarded. Look for used desks in flea markets or at the Salvation Army. Or check a children's furniture store or mail order supply for a new one. Children think it's "awesome" to have a desk of their own. If you can't find a desk, or space is a problem, set up a corner of your kitchen counter or part of a shelf as a writing area for your child.

**You'll Need**
unlined paper; pencils, crayons, markers; note pads; folders, rubber stamps of letters and words, envelopes, postage stamps (optional)

**What to Do**

1 Tell your child that you're setting aside a place for her to do her writing. Show her the place.

2 Talk about the things that people use when they write. Work with your child to make a list of the things she needs. Start with the basics: paper and pencil. Add other items to the list if you wish.

3 Take your child and the list to the store. Let your child help you find all the items on the list.

4 Help your child find places to keep her writing things in, or near, her writing place.

5 If you have similar things, mark your child's with her name.

6 Show your child how to do necessary tasks like sharpening pencils, erasing, and pushing the button on a mechanical pencil to make the lead come up.

7 Disappear. Leave your child to explore, experiment, produce, and publish by bringing the product to you for discussion.

**Follow-up Activities**
- When your child finishes writing, encourage her to sort her things out and put them away: pencils together, crayons together, paper in the paper basket. And let her make the decision as to what to do with her products: throw out, hang, mail, store.
- Give your child writing supplies as gifts, finding as many interesting items as you can.

**What's Happening**

There's a place for bathing, there's a place for sleeping, there's a place for eating. Writing is just one more thing we do all the time, so your child needs a place set up to do that. And just as soap and washcloths are found near the tub, we have writing materials in their proper place. It's no big deal. It's just an everyday activity. Doesn't everybody have a place to write? How the world would change if they did!

**Moving Ahead**

Help your child set up a folder and file system for her work, or create a portfolio for artwork and writing. Let your child dictate what goes where. This is another way to work sorting into your routine and to encourage your child to set up systems of organization.

**Helpful Hint**

Consider a hard plastic pencil case or soft plastic or fabric zipper case to store your child's pencils, crayons, and markers. Your child will enjoy dumping them out to sort, and they can be easily transported to waiting rooms, cars, and other writing places. Keep a notebook in your pocket or in your child's backpack, and you complete the portable writing outfit.

# 14 Unique Units

*Help your child see, as Rudyard Kipling did,*
*"The world is so full of a number of things . . ."*

**Before You Begin**
Start by getting together a big pile of stuff. Here, I give the example of using cups and spoons as a unit for study. You can create a unit out of anything that's of interest to your child. This activity works well outside.

**You'll Need**
an assortment of spoons, cups, other scooping implements; two large bowls; things to scoop up (sand, rice, water, flour, pudding, and so on)

**What to Do**
1 Lay the spoons, cups, and one or two other scooping materials on a table. Invite your child to explore these items.

2 Ask your child to tell you about what he's doing. Talk about his actions and get his impression of how he feels while he's doing each thing.

3 With your child, compare one spoon or cup to another. Compare the cups to the spoons. Talk about them: Which is heavier? Lighter? Easier to use?

4 Provide two large bowls. Fill one with water, rice, or flour. Have your child experiment with moving the material from one bowl to another with different cups and spoons. Invite him to tell you what he's doing as he does this.

**Follow-up Activities**
• Talk about other ways you can experiment with spoons or cups. Show your child how to breathe on the spoon and get it to stick to his nose (handle end down). Show him his reflection on the front and back of the spoon. Place one spoon in a bowl of other spoons of different kinds and ask your child to find it.

- Work with your child to set up Polaroid photographs of his spoon experiments and to label them. Or have your child draw one of his spoon experiments and tell about it.

**What's Happening**   This activity gives your child the opportunity to explore and get the hang of using one kind of tool: a spoon or cup. By making available an assortment of similar tools, you invite your child to compare, sort, and differentiate between them based on size, function, appearance, and other attributes. When you talk to your child about his explorations, you encourage him to use language to describe, predict, and analyze. And you guide your child to use his hands in a certain way for a certain purpose, as he does in writing.

**Moving Ahead**   Expand the unit idea to many areas. You can have a sewing unit, in which you assemble an assortment of needles, thread, pins, and fabric, and test them out. You can have a screwing unit, in which you gather all sorts of nuts, bolts, and screws, wood with drilled holes and nail-started holes, and a few screwdrivers, then go to it! Let your child be both apprentice and expert, and talk about what you discover as you go.

**Helpful Hints**
- Have your child keep a notebook of his experiences with particular tools. He can draw or trace each tool and write about it in invented writing.
- If you're doing something hardware-oriented, pick up a hardware store circular and cut out pictures of tools from it that are like the ones you're using.
- Visit a houseware store and check out all the cups and spoons.

# 15 Radio, Radio

*The little bit of background music you turn on may seem like just so much noise to your child, until you help him tune in.*

**H**elps develop: *purposeful listening, auditory discrimination, observation skills, vocabulary*

**Before You Begin**
Have a reason for turning on the radio, and tell your child what the reason is: "How about a little music?" or "I need to hear the weather report" or "I wonder if there are any traffic jams ahead." This will involve your child in listening with you.

**You'll Need**
a radio; a tape recorder or CD player (optional)

**What to Do**

**1** Turn on the radio. Tune it in. Tell your child why you're choosing this station: "They play great jazz, and I thought you'd like it." Or "This is the station with the traffic report." If you just want some background music, run through the stations, and let your child choose with you.

**2** Listen together. Make comments now and then to guide your child's ears: "Okay, here comes the weather. Let's see if they say rain." or "Hey! The Beatles! Listen for the part where they sing . . ."

**3** Recap what you listen to together. "Hey, they said snow!" or "Mm, I love that song." Act on the information you get from the radio, when appropriate. Head to the grocery store for hot chocolate to drink during the coming snowstorm. Or move to another medium: "That sounded like an interesting news story. They'll have pictures in the newspaper tonight. We'll have to look."

**Follow-up Activities**

- Talk about the ads you hear. If you pass by a business that was advertised on the radio, point it out to your child. Sing the jingle.

- Note music that comes on the radio that you have on tape or CD at home. Point out that radio stations have record, tape, and CD collections too.

- Talk about what you like and dislike about what you hear.

**What's Happening**  *Have you ever tried to listen to a radio broadcast in a foreign language? It can be very confusing. There is no context, no frame of reference (on TV you can at least tell who's talking and make guesses about the topic by looking at the visuals). Even though your child speaks English, the radio is adult speech, fast-paced and out of context. By clueing your child in to what the people are talking about, you open a door into this mode of communication. You're also helping your child develop confidence in her ability to listen for specific information. Take what you hear and apply it to your life and your actions, and you create another link between language and life.*

**Moving Ahead**  Encourage your child to create her own radio broadcasts. Make up a weather report you'd prefer to the one you just heard. Give the news of the day (in your home, school, or town) in radio style. Fake a microphone or use a real one. Keep the broadcast on tape.

**Helpful Hints**
- Talk about how radio signals reach your radio through sound waves and antennas. Keep it simple: invisible signals tell the radio what sounds to make, and antennas help pass the signals along like hands passing things.
- Visit (or drive by and point out) a local radio station.
- Call your radio station to let your child request a song or to listen as you do.
- Take apart an old radio with your child. Point out (or use a book to figure out) the functions of the parts inside.

# PART TWO

# Mainly Reading

Reading is the process of making meaning out of symbols. A child who points to the golden arches and crows, "McDonald's!" is reading. So is the child who holds a familiar book in his hand and retells the story. And so, of course, is the child who looks at a three-letter word and sounds out the word *cat*. But none of them is reading fluently. How do you help your child to reach that goal?

The first step in encouraging your child to blossom as a reader is to accept his reading at whatever level, *right now*. When a toddler takes his first step, parents say, "He's walking!" When your child picks up a book or interprets letters or symbols on a sign, say, "He's reading!"

The second step is to expose your child to many ways that written language is used, so that he will see reading as a necessary tool for getting along in the world, as a joy and a pleasure, and as an ordinary part of life. This section focuses on specific experiences that will involve your child more closely in reading.

# 16 **Match It Up!**

**H**elps develop: *visual, auditory, and other sensory matching skills, and categorization skills*

*Which ones go together?*
*Which ones are different?*

**Before You Begin**   Here you'll provide two sets of objects and have your child match them up, focusing on a particular sense. As an example, I'll use a game that focuses on the sense of touch.

**You'll Need**   an assortment of ten materials with different textures: fabric, wood, tile, screening, etc.; 4- by 6-inch index cards; a shoe box; glue

**What to Do**

**1** Cut two 2-inch (5-centimeter) squares of each of the ten materials, for a total of twenty squares.

**2** Cut a hole in the lid of a shoe box, large enough for a hand to fit in. Tape the lid onto the box. Place one set of squares—one square of each kind of material—in the box.

**3** Glue the remaining squares onto the index cards, 5 squares to each card.

**4** Give your child one of the index cards. Hold one yourself.

**5** Ask your child to reach into the shoe box and pick up a square. With her hand still in the box, ask her to feel the square to see if it matches one of those on her card. If she's not sure, have her pull the square out, look at it, and compare it to those on the card.

**6** If it matches one on her card, have her place the square on top of the one on her card. If it doesn't match, have her return it to the box.

**7** Take your turn putting your hand into the box and holding a square. Talk about what you feel. Describe the textures. Compare aloud. *Think* aloud. Encourage your child to use language to explain her findings too.

**8** Continue the game until both of you have covered all your squares. (I prefer to make this game noncompetitive.)

**Follow-up Activity**　　Once you've established names for each kind of material (see Step 7), try giving one name and inviting your child to find it by touch.

**Moving Ahead**　　Here are a few ways to raise the level of the activity.

- Use only fabric, rather than an assortment of materials.
- Work together on one card. Have one person reach into the box and describe the feeling of a square. Have the other person examine the card to see if one of the squares there matches the one described.
- Place magnet letters in the box and attach matching magnet letters to the card with glue or double-sided tape. Let your child try to match letters by feeling them.

**Helpful Hint**　　Here are some ideas for using this game to develop other senses.

- Taste: match flavored lollipops with the fruits they're meant to taste like.
- Smell: Match cotton pads soaked in different essences (vanilla, vinegar, peppermint extract, alcohol) with the bottles they come from.
- Hearing: Use a tape recorder to match sounds with pictures. For example: a meow with a picture of a cat. (There are games like this on the market, but it's fun to make your own.)
- Sight: Match playing cards, photographs, company logos.

# 17 Shape Finder

AROUND THE HOUSE

**H**elps develop: *visual matching, classification of objects, symbolic representation of three-dimensional objects*

*Does your child realize that shapes she sees on paper exist in the world around us?*

**Before You Begin**
Find a few minutes to make this game when your child isn't around. One quick way to assess your child's level and to adapt to it is to involve him in making another game with you after he tries the first one.

**You'll Need**
building blocks and toys in various shapes and sizes; a book of blank paper; pencil; shoe box

**What to Do**
1 Choose four or five blocks or toys.
2 Trace each object on a page of a blank book, one per page.
3 Store the toys or blocks in a shoe box.
4 Show your child the book and the full shoe box. Encourage your child to match the objects in the box to the shapes on the pages.

**Follow-up Activities**
- Talk to your child about the pictures. How does he think you made them?
- Get your child involved in tracing shapes and blocks (or suggesting ones for you to trace) in the book.
- Take turns matching shapes with objects. Talk about what you're thinking as you match an object with its traced shape: describe the shape, the number of sides, the rough line that suggests hair on a doll, and other distinguishing features. Fit the object inside the traced line to confirm the match.

54

*Matching a two-dimensional drawing to a three-dimensional object is hard. It's a big step up from matching two three-dimensional objects or even two two-dimensional drawings. By sharing this game with your child you give him the opportunity to understand many things—the relationship between the physical world and the world that appears on paper, the attributes of things that place them in one category or another, and the translation from the language of 3-D to the language of 2-D: line* vs. *shape, curved* vs. *round,* etc. *Understanding that a two-dimensional drawing is a symbolic representation of a real thing is a step toward comprehending that written words stand for objects, actions, and ideas.*

**Moving Ahead**

Eventually you'll be able to write *doll* on a piece of paper and have your child find the doll in the box. The drawing is the first step. Make this game more difficult—and global—by drawing shapes in the book and having your child locate them on a walk through town, the mall, or an office building. Where are the triangles? The right angles? The hexagons? Talk about similarities and differences, the attributes that place each object and drawing firmly in the same category.

**Helpful Hint**

You can make the outline of an object more evident by using the side of a piece of chalk or a crayon to shade a broad margin around the object instead of merely tracing a line.

# 18 Cutting Coupons

*Helps develop: matching, linking writing with life, classification*

*You and your child can have countless reading adventures while you get your shopping done!*

**Before You Begin**  Do you already have a coupon file? If you do, show your child how to use it. If you don't, set up a file with your child. Together, decide on a system for filing the coupons. Will you group items by type? By the aisle where they're found in your store?

**You'll Need**  coupon circulars; your grocery list; scissors; pencil; a box for the coupons

**What to Do**  
1 Go through the coupon circular from your local store and/or newspaper with your child. Read the names of the products aloud and talk about what they are.

2 Talk about the purpose of coupons: to save money, to encourage people to buy certain products.

3 Ask your child to help you identify things you already buy or might buy. Consult your grocery list. Involve your child in decisions about which brand, color, or flavor to buy.

4 Help your child clip and file the coupons you plan to use.

5 Hit the store! Take your purchases to the checkout counter. Talk with your child about the savings from the coupons. One way to show this to your child is to have the grocer return cash to you for your coupons. Even if your grocer is unwilling to do this, the cash register receipt will usually show you what you saved on your total bill. Point out the amount saved to your child.

**Follow-up Activities**
- Write your grocery list with your child. Send her to the cupboard to check the cereal supply, to the vegetable bin to check how many carrots are left, to the bathroom to see if the toothpaste tube is nearly empty.
- Hand your child a coupon in the appropriate aisle and help her find the matching item.

**What's Happening**

*Instead of just bringing your child along as you shop, you're making her an active participant in the shopping process. You're also connecting written words and graphics with real-life foods and experiences. Talk about the reasons that you buy things, the advertising methods that go into encouraging your purchase through coupons, and the words, numbers, and symbols on the coupons.*

**Moving Ahead**

When a container of food is finished, help your child to notice which items are thrown out and which items are saved for recycling. Give your child tasks to do with you.

**Helpful Hints**
- An index card box with dividers is ideal for storing coupons. The dividers can be used to create pictorial or written labels for the sections, and the box is easy for your child to carry. Your child can help you decide whether to group items by aisle, type, or some other method.
- Here's something I do to help myself that may help you and your child, too: if there's a brand or version of a product that I like but can't recall easily, I'll bring the empty container to the store and match it up.

# 19 Laundry Soap

*"Bigger! Brighter! Bolder! Better!" What does advertising language—including the small print on packages— actually mean in our lives?*

**Before You Begin**

Talk to your child about the advertising language he hears when he watches television or listens to the radio. This activity gives you a chance to start your child reading such language and investigating it closely.

**You'll Need**

a bottle or box (or two or three) of laundry detergent; dirty laundry (it's always available in most households)

**What to Do**

**1** Go to the grocery store with your child when you need laundry detergent. Together, look at the choices and read the labels.

**2** Talk about the words on the boxes and cartons. They use such amazing language, don't they? Talk about the promises. Can they really be true? Compare colors, type-faces, and other visuals on the packaging. Talk about which package is most attractive to you and your child.

**3** Read the ingredients to your child. Ask questions. Are any of them familiar? What do you think they contribute?

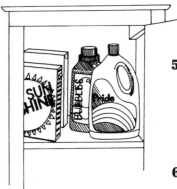

**4** Zero in on vocabulary. *Biodegradable.* What does that mean? *Scented. Non-scented.* Do we need the scented one? *Safe for septic systems.* So what's a septic system?

**5** Read the directions. Does the process require presoaking? Rinsing? Adding bleach? Adding fabric softener? Discuss with your child the process of getting laundry clean, step-by-step. Compare the directions on a few different products. Are there pictures to illustrate? Which process is the easiest? The most complicated?

**6** Together, choose one kind of detergent. Then go home and use it to do the laundry together.

**Follow-up Activity**   Compare the new product to your old detergent. Compare it to other new products. Are there differences in smell? In feel? In stain removal? In overall result?

**What's Happening**   *Through this activity you bring your child into an adult realm of using print for information. You're showing your child a way that people use language to shape their actions and affect their lives. You're demonstrating and defining some amazing adjectives and complicated-sounding terms, and you're modeling how to follow directions through actions. You're giving your child a part in a household process, in making decisions based on words, and in understanding the motivations behind advertising language and packaging.*

**Moving Ahead**   Apply the same principles and practices to other products: snack foods, dairy products, paint, and so on. What's in them? What do they say they will do? Can they really do that? Let's pass. Or, let's try this one and see.

**Helpful Hint**   Duplicate one of the stain-removal tests shown on television to compare one product with another. See Activity 9: The Terrific Tube.

# 20 A Passion for Words

**H**elps develop: increased vocabulary, ability to connect language with life, ability to categorize

*Before I knew four-year-old Sam, any orange truck was a steam shovel to me. Now I know backhoes, bulldozers, front-end loaders . . . Your child can remember all kinds of complicated words if the subject fascinates him.*

**Before You Begin**    Ask your child, "Is there something you want to know more about?" You may already be aware (and well aware) of something that holds a great interest for your child. This is an activity that arises when a child demonstrates a fascination with part of the world around her.

**You'll Need**    a child with an interest; a library book that relates to the interest; your own vast vocabulary

**What to Do**
1 Encourage your child to ask questions about a topic that interests her.

2 Don't be an answer machine. Instead, cock your head and say, "I wonder how we can find out the answer to that?"

3 Spend time observing or studying the thing your child is interested in. If it's a construction site, for example, schedule time to stop and watch the work. If it's ants, plan a half hour to watch some ants. You could even buy an ant farm for closer, more constant observation.

4 Discuss what your child observes. Use new words about the topic: *excavation, tunnel, concrete, vibration.*

**Follow-up Activities**
• Help your child find an expert on the topic. If it's ants, visit a nature center and talk to someone there about ants. If it's a construction site your child is fascinated with, encourage her to talk to the workers.

• Have your child draw pictures and write about her interest.

- Go to the library or bookstore and find a book about the topic. With your child, go through the process of locating a book, determining whether it has the information you want, and buying or borrowing it.
- Use a camera to document the observation.
- Help your child use photographs, pictures, and writing to create a book about her interest.

**What's Happening**

*You're following your child's lead, giving her ideas about how to find out more about her interests, and, most important, taking her seriously. Children's author and illustrator Tomie de Paola fondly recalls the studio his parents set up for him when he was four years old and told them he wanted to be an artist. De Paola—and all children—read this sort of response as affirmation. Someone is saying, "Of course you know who you are. Of course you will be, know, do. Here, let me give you the tools you'll need to do it." What a wonderful gift!*

*When you share vocabulary with a child, you help her to organize the world into ever-expanding categories. Once Sam's mother gave him the words* backhoe *and* front-end loader, *he never called them steam shovels again; he looked to see which one it was. Sam already knew the difference through observation. Imagine his thrill when he learned the words to describe the difference.*

**Moving Ahead**

Take your child with you when you need to get information at the bank, library, or pharmacy. Encourage her to listen to your questions, to help with your research, and to learn the vocabulary you use. What's a card catalog? What's Infotrack? What are antihistamines? What's a C.D. account? And so on. It's the stuff of life. Share it!

**Helpful Hint**

The library has many books in the picture book and language section (400s in the Dewey Decimal System) that show labeled objects. Try Richard Scarry's books or the *First 1000 Words* series.

# 21 Poetry in Motion

**H**elps develop: rhythm, memory through listening, speaking, seeing patterns in words

*The dame made a curtsey,*
*The dog made a bow,*
*The dame said, "Your servant,"*
*The dog said, "Bow! Wow!"*

**Before You Begin**   Share a rhyme or two with your child. Recite it, read it, talk about the illustrations in the book beside it, repeat it often, learn it together. This activity is a tool for learning a rhyme and using it to learn more about written language.

**You'll Need**   Mother Goose rhymes, or other poems and songs in books or recordings; large sheets of paper; crayons or markers

**What to Do**
1 Choose a rhyme or song with your child. You might ask, "Which song (or rhyme or poem) is your favorite today? Which one should we write and hang up?"
2 Have the child recite the poem or help you remember what comes next as you write it on a large sheet of paper.
3 Have your child illustrate the poem if he wants to.
4 Together choose a place to post your poem.

**Follow-up Activities**
- Recite the poem together. Use the poster as your reminder.
- Keep your large-sized paper handy. Let your child suggest additional poems or songs to record and hang up. Keep them all on the wall, or replace with new ones, and file old ones away for your child to look through at will.

**What's Happening**   *By writing down a poem that a child can say all or part of, you make it an important thing, an event. A child who looks at a poster of words and recites a poem is reading—and one who dictates a rhyme to you while you inscribe it is writing. Again, you're linking written words to your everyday life as you enhance that life with rhythm, rhymes, and music. Nursery rhymes of one kind or another are used to comfort, interest, and communicate with children in almost every culture. And, of course, each society has its own music, poetry, and popular literature. When you share this with your child, you bring him into literary society.*

**Moving Ahead**   Find a rhyming poem to read aloud with your child. Stop speaking after the next-to-last word of each line and let your child speak the last word as you point to it. He'll do so from memory, and hearing his own voice associated with the word your finger points to will help him to associate the spoken word with the written one. Doing it with the last word helps focus on the similar sounds and spellings of rhyming words, leading him to make generalizations about sound and spelling.

**Helpful Hint**   Try these books of poems and songs:
- *Raffi Singable Songbook* by Ken Raffi (Crown)
- *When We Were Very Young* by A. A.. Milne (Dutton)
- *The Earth Is Painted Green: A Garden of Poems About Our Planet* edited by Barbara Brenner (Scholastic)
- *The Baby's Bedtime Book* by Kay Chorao (Dutton)
- *Where the Sidewalk Ends* by Shel Silverstein (HarperCollins)

# 22 Drivin' Around Readin'

**H**elps develop: connections between culture and language, visual matching

*You can get your kicks on Route 66—and your child can learn to read there too.*

**Before You Begin** You can work up to this activity with a very young child by pointing things out as you pass by on a walk or in a car: restaurants, fire stations, etc. She'll begin to differentiate between houses and places of business, gas stations and eating places, before she notes their signs. She's making her own meaning, interpreting what she sees in her own way. When she starts to identify individual fast-food joints or the grocery store, she's ready for this activity.

**You'll Need** a road with signs

**What to Do** 1 Invite your child: "I'll bet you can read a sign on this road."

2 Wait for her to identify a gas station, Pizza Hut, or the girl with braids on the Wendy's sign. Say, "Great reading!" even if it's clear that architecture, rather than letters, was the main clue.

3 Read other signs with your child and ask her to point out more.

4 Talk about the signs along the road as if they were news: "Look! They're having a sale at the art supply store. See the big red 'Sale' sign? Maybe we should look for markers." Another way is to talk about what you're doing when you're driving: "Hmm, this sign says 'Three miles to exit.' I wonder how long it'll take us to get there?"

Talk about how things got their names and about what the names mean. "I wonder why they call it Pizza Hut. A hut is a tiny little house. What do you think?" Or discuss where the names come from. "Unquowa Road. The Unquowa were people who lived here a long time ago. I wonder what life was like here then?"

**What's Happening**

*Language is a tool for expressing ideas and sharing information. Most children in a society as rich in words and graphics as ours will pick up on this activity naturally. You can guide them into greater understanding by discussing the words, how they're used, where they're located, and why they're written and placed as they are. You can encourage children to become involved with language just by noticing it. Often parents go about their business, toting children along, without explaining their actions, not realizing how far a little explanation would go. Tell your child what you're looking at when you're following directions on a highway or seeking out an office or store, and you'll give valuable insight into the practical uses of reading. And you'll get help, too!*

**Moving Ahead** Use signs in all the ways you can think of. Make a game of looking for all the *A*s. Talk about pictures and characters on the signs too. Discuss why all the fast-food places and gas stations have such eye-catching signs. Which signs do you like best?

**Helpful Hint** Work with your child to make signs for your home. Cut letters from advertisements to form the words, or simply come up with a picture symbol that stands for each room or area. Label the signs, hang them up, and have your child take you on a tour to read them.

# 23 Rhymes on Stage

**H**elps develop: ability to link words to action, ability to respond to oral direction, dramatic play

*Want to make a story or rhyme come alive for your child? Stage it!*

**Before You Begin**    This activity goes above and beyond "I'm a Little Teapot" by asking children to create their own movements to go along with familiar rhymes and songs. Think of the rhymes and songs your child already knows. Decide on two or three that would be simple to dramatize. Or use the examples below if you know them.

**You'll Need**    space inside or outside for performing; nursery rhymes, songs, or simple stories

**What to Do**    1  Ask your child to help you act out a rhyme or song.  As an example, act out something he knows. You be Miss Muffet, and let your child be the spider. Say the rhyme aloud as you both play your parts.

> Little Miss Muffet sat on a tuffet
> *(Sit with a "bowl" in your hand)*
>
> Eating her curds and whey
> *(mime eating with a spoon)*
>
> Along came a spider
> *(child comes creeping in)*
>
> And sat down beside her
> *(child rubs up against you)*
>
> And frightened Miss Muffet away
> *(run away shrieking)*

**2** Now suggest acting out another story or rhyme with several children. Or have a child suggest one. It's fun to use a story or poem with a few characters.

> Five green and speckled frogs sat on a speckled log
> *(children sit in a row)*
>
> Eating some most delicious bugs
> *(children rub their tummies and say:)* Yum, yum!
>
> One jumped into the pool, where it was nice and cool
> *(one child jumps away)*
>
> Then there were four green speckled frogs
> *(children say:)* Glub! Glub!

**Follow-up Activity**    Make it more complicated by having a child act out a familiar story while you read it or tell it. If you have additional children, give them parts to play. Or help your child stage the story with stuffed animals, dolls, or puppets. Here's an example:

> Once upon a time in a house in the forest lived the three bears *(child pats three bears on the head)*.
>
> One was a Papa bear *(child acts him out)*. One was a Mama bear *(child acts her out)*. One was a wee bear *(child acts him out)*.
>
> One day they were walking, and as they were walking *(child mimes walking)*,
>
> Along came a girl with long hair *(child pretends to brush out long hair)*
>
> Her name was Goldilocks, upon the door she knocks *(child taps on something—knock knock knock)*
>
> But no one was there *(child shrugs)*
>
> So she went inside! . . .

---

*What's Happening*    It's beautifully simple. Your child is listening to or reciting words found in a book and turning them into tangible, visible action. Characters become real. Rhythms are expressed physically. And when your child participates in this game with you and/or other children, she learns what it means to adapt, collaborate, rehearse, revise, and perform.

**Moving Ahead**   Have your child narrate a story, while you be the actor in it. "Once there was a girl named Nathalie who liked to climb on rocks. One day while she was climbing, a bird came along and landed beside her . . ." Invent the story with your child or encourage her to act what happens next while you think of appropriate narration.

**Helpful Hint**   You can make a picture chart to help your child recall the dramatic action you improvise together. Use the guidelines in Activity 7: Take This Job and Chart It to sketch out your story, song, or rhyme.

# 24 What Would You Do If You Were...Who?

**H**elps develop: connection between literature and life, dramatic play, storytelling

*What would Curious George do if he were here?*

**Before You Begin** Start this activity during a moment when you're hanging out with your child. You're out in the yard or in line at the bank, the delicatessen, or the museum. Use this conversation-starter to take you through the line, out the door, and all the way home again.

**You'll Need** any interesting situation; two vivid imaginations: yours and your child's

**What to Do**

1 Think of a character from a book. Ask your child, "What would ——— do if she were here?" Ask your child to imagine that he's a character from a favorite story, in the place where you are now. The character could be someone curious (Curious George), devious (the Big Bad Wolf), gloomy (Eeyore), creative (Little Bear), or inventive (the Cat in the Hat).

2 Encourage your child to consider what the character is like and why she or he is likely to do what the child suggests.

3 If you can, act out or play out through dialogue the scene that might take place. Encourage your child to add to or alter the scene by asking leading questions. "So, you think that Charlotte the spider would hang out in the mobile if she came to the museum. What would she think of the fountain?"

**Follow-up Activity**  Suggest, or have your child suggest to you, another character. What would this character do in the same situation? How do this character's actions differ from the first character's, and why?

**What's Happening**  *You and your child are making book characters your own. You're helping your child understand character: clear personality, likes and dislikes, typical actions. And you're exploring these ideas by placing the character in new settings and providing him or her with new situations to work through. It's similar to the process any author undertakes in starting a new book about a pre-existing character: coming up with an idea that's interesting for his character, trying out a plot line and carrying it to its end, evaluating it, revising it, and starting all over if needed. What's more, you're encouraging your child to put someone else in his own place and imagine how another person (or creature) would deal with the same situation. It's a terrific mind and heart stretcher for anyone.*

**Moving Ahead**  If you like your story well enough, retell it with your child, or have him write it down. Act it out together and/or record it.

**Helpful Hint**  Use a copy machine to make small cards with pictures of characters from your child's favorite books. Keep this deck of ten or so cards in your pocket or give them to your child to carry. Whip them out at opportune moments. Ask your child to "pick a card, any card." Then improvise a scene on the spot, starring the character on the card.

# 25 At Your Command

*Charades for beginners makes words the impetus for your child's action.*

**Helps develop:** *reading, writing, matching movements with words*

**Before You Begin**    Prepare a pile of action words such as *jump, run, dance, sing, hide, peek, hop, clap, sleep, spin.* Write each word on a separate piece of paper. For very young children, draw a stick figure doing the action required, and write the word under the drawing. For beginning readers, write the words only. Children might also write the commands themselves in invented writing.

**You'll Need**    paper; pencil; bowl *or* bag

**What to Do**

1 Show your child one paper and describe the game.

2 Fold the papers and place them in the bowl or bag.

3 Have your child pull a paper from the bowl and read it silently.

4 Ask the child to act out the command on the paper.

5 Try to guess what the word on the paper is by watching your child.

6 Take turns until all the papers have been pulled. You can also keep putting them back in the bag and play until everyone has had enough.

**Moving Ahead**    Increase the difficulty of this game by using complete sentences ("Sit on the bed") or words with more letters or syllables. Move up, eventually, to adult-style charades, in which players act out phrases, names, and titles through breaking down syllables into sounds and images. Instead of using movie titles, use your child's favorite book titles or characters.

**Helpful Hint**    Have children work in pairs to read and act out commands. Two heads are better than one!

# 26 Rhymin' Around

*"It rhymes if it has the same ending."*
—Bethany, age six

**Before You Begin**  If you haven't already been reading your child poems and/or nursery rhymes, begin. Then show your child how to play this rhyme game, and you may find yourself playing it every time you're in transit.

**You'll Need**  you and your child; pencil and paper

**What to Do**  1  Ask your child to pick a word, any word. For example: *ball*.

2  Find a rhyme for your child's word. For example: *ball, fall*.

3  Now ask your child to find another rhyme for the same word: *ball, fall, shawl*. (At first your child's rhymes may not be real words. It doesn't matter! In fact, it's better. He's still rhyming—that is, he's changing the initial sound and keeping the end the same.)

4  Keep rhyming the same word until you and your child can't think of any more rhymes for it.

**Follow-up Activity**  Come up with a really long list (more than six) of words that rhyme. Get excited about it. "Wow! I never thought we could think of so many rhyming words!" As soon as you have access to pencil and paper, make a list of those words with your child. Say, "I really want to remember this great list. Tell me the words, will you?" Then let your child watch as you write the words down. *Don't discuss spelling.* The point of this list is to demonstrate, not to explain, the relationships between words that rhyme. Let your child draw his own conclusions, in his own time, that endings of words that rhyme are often, but not always, spelled the same: *rough, stuff.*

**What's Happening**    Through rhymes your child comes to the understanding that a word, like a story , has a beginning, a middle, and an end. Creating a rhyme for a word is a way of manipulating it, changing its beginning. It focuses attention on a single sound, the starting or initial sound, and eventually on the letter that makes that sound. Humans like rhythms and patterns, so rhyming is a particularly fun game to play. Your child will enjoy thinking of words to stump you: what rhymes with orange?

**Moving Ahead**    Work with your child to write couplets, pairs of rhyming sentences such as the one Bethany, the child quoted at the beginning of this activity, invented about her dog:

> He's happy as a clam
> To just be who he am.

Never mind the grammar. The point is that you invite your child to use rhythm and rhyme in his own way, for his own purposes.

**Helpful Hint**    I'm against using books to teach about rhymes and spelling. Rather, once your child has grasped the concept that there's a relationship between sounds and spelling, read a few rhyming books with him. These are designed specifically to point up the sound/spelling relationship.

- *Hop on Pop* by Dr. Seuss (Random House)
- *Green Eggs and Ham* by Dr. Seuss (Random House)
- *Go, Dog, Go* by P. D. Eastman (Random House)

# 27 Fonts of Knowledge

27

**H**elps develop: *print literacy, visual matching, letter recognition*

*Help your child see that a letter means the same thing whether it's written fancy or plain.*

**Before You Begin**
Show your child how to get into the word processing program on your computer. Some parents understandably don't want their children to do this by themselves; still, it's good for the child to see how the computer's "brain" works. Give her time to experiment with the various keys, to fiddle around, writing in invented writing. Show her how the shift key works, how to save and print. The point of this activity is to show your child different typefaces or fonts. It helps if she already has a handle on the function of the word processor.

**You'll Need**
a computer with a word processing program that has various styles (italic; bold) and typefaces

**What to Do**
1 Ask your child to choose a word or other series of letters (a sentence, the alphabet, her name) to type into the computer. For a younger child, start with just one letter or let her "scribble"—tap out random letters.

2 Print her work out. Talk about how the printout looks different from the screen.

3 Show your child how to change the letters to a new font.

4 Talk about how the new font is different from the old font. Boldface? Italics? Serifs? No serifs? (Serifs are the little accenting lines at the ends of the strokes of a letter that this typeface has, such as at the bottom of the *A*.)

5 Have your child type a little more. Print her work out.

**Follow-up Activities**

- Tell your child the names of the different fonts. Discuss how they might have gotten their names. For example: Chicago, Parisian, New York, Times, Courier.

- Try more fonts. Come up with a sample of all the fonts on your computer by typing the same letter or word in each font.

**What's Happening**

As your child reads more and more books, signs, and other literature, she'll encounter many different typefaces, fonts, and methods of penmanship that may be confusing. It's a good idea to help her see that there are many ways of forming a letter and that the letter itself doesn't change in definition or usage.

**Moving Ahead**

Create your own font with your child. Form letters out of construction paper, knives and forks, blocks on the floor. Are these still letters? You bet! Older children like to create their own personalized fonts, using graph paper to get the size uniform. If you have a scanner for your computer, you can get these fonts into your computer for your child's use.

**Helpful Hint**

With your child, study a type catalog to see all the ways that letters are written. You can find these in art supply, stationery, or business supply stores, or print shops.

# 28 Books Open the Door to Feelings

**H**elps develop: empathy, connection between words and feelings, understanding of character and plot, cause and effect

*How does it feel to be a fat Pooh-bear,*
*stuck in the door of Rabbit's House,*
*with Rabbit's tea towels hanging on your feet to dry?*

**Before You Begin**  Have your child select a familiar book. You can do so much more with it than simply reading what's there.

**You'll Need**  storybooks, picture books

**What to Do**
1 As you're reading the book, stop at an illustration.
2 Talk about what the picture shows and how it adds to the story.
3 Ask your child about what's going on in the illustration. "What's happening? Why? What's going to happen next?"
4 Focus some questions on the characters. "Who's this? What's she doing? How do you think she's feeling? What do you think she'll do if she meets the wolf?" Talk about their stances and facial expressions. "I wonder what she's thinking."
5 Go on reading. If the text specifically names an emotion, talk about that word and why the character is feeling that way. "It says he's furious. What do you think that means? What's making him feel that way? What's he going to do about it?"
6 Discuss how a character's feelings evolve over the course of the story. "Do you think he's still mad? What happened to change his feelings?"

**Follow-up Activities**
- Talk about how one character's actions affect the feelings of another. How does one character comfort another who's sad? What causes someone to get angry, to feel left out, to cry or yell?
- Ask your child to relate to someone in the plot. "What would you do if you were there? What would you say to Cinderella to make her feel better?"

**What's Happening**

By reading about the feelings of others and analyzing why they feel that way, how they show their feelings, and how they resolve conflicts of feeling, children gain understanding of themselves and develop strategies for dealing with their feelings. One of the most important functions of language is to allow us to name things—and feelings can be some of the hardest things to name. Through words, pictures, and gentle discussion, children learn to identify strong emotions and to empathize with others.

**Moving Ahead**

Find ways to weave stories into discussions of feelings in your child's life. "I'm as full as Pooh was when he tried to leave Rabbit's house!" or "Remember how Little Bear felt when Emily went home at the end of the summer? That's how I'm feeling about Grandma leaving." Not only will you give a new dimension to your feelings and your child's, you'll help him draw parallels between his life and the lives of others. As he remembers a story, he may find comfort, he may think of ideas about ways to help himself and others, and he may feel a stronger link to the books you share together.

**Helpful Hint**

Do a study of people's faces with your child. Explore the pages of a magazine, a photo exhibition, or (surreptitiously) the faces of people on the bus or subway. What might be the feeling—and the story—behind each face?

# 29 Organic Words

**H**elps develop: ability to read words, understanding of the purpose of writing, connection between written words and life

*Some words get stuck in your mind. It's the same for your child. If you write them down for her, they'll be hers to keep forever—or, if she chooses, to throw away.*

**Before You Begin**    Listen to your child talk as he plays. Is there one word that comes up often? Children—and other people—get fixated on individual words which for them are organic: that is, having innate worth (the term *organic words* comes from Sylvia Ashton-Warner, a ground-breaking teacher). Here, they are just one way we help children to see the uses of language and also to get some of their words out of their heads and onto paper.

**You'll Need**    index cards *or* small pad; pencil; rubber band

**What to Do**    **1** Show your child the index cards or the pad.

**2** Tell your child that the cards are to keep important words on. Say, "Is there a word you would like me to write?"

**3** Write any word your child suggests on a card. Write clearly, in printing.

**4** Give the card to your child to keep. Give him a rubber band to keep them together.

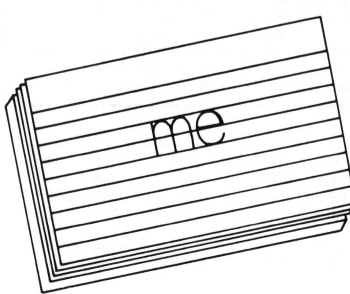

**Follow-up Activities**

- Keep blank cards handy. Tell your child that you'll write any word he wants, any time.

- Follow the child's lead in choosing and discussing the words, their meaning, their use, and their spelling. Talk about what your child wants to talk about. *Don't use the words to demonstrate or test spelling.*

- Have your child read through his words now and then. Help him at first, if necessary.

- Suggest words that relate to new situations that are of particular interest to your child. Suppose your child has pinkeye. Take advantage of the opportunity to give your child the word *conjunctivitis,* the scientific name for his condition.

- Be prepared to write almost any word the child suggests, to talk about the context in which the child hears and understands the word, and to avoid making judgments about the word or its context.

**What's Happening**

*The idea that naming something gives you power over it goes back to the most ancient folklore. Names—and indeed all words are names—have power. When you hear a child admit, "I'm afraid of the dark," he's doing something great: naming an unspeakable fear. How much more powerful is writing a word on a piece of paper and keeping it inside one's pocket. Don't be surprised if your child's word list includes some powerful items. The purpose here is not to teach reading, writing, or spelling through use of important organic words, but to show one of the most vital uses of the written word: possession of an idea. It's necessary for parents, then, to put aside their own opinions of the word involved and to make themselves available as scribes.*

**Moving Ahead**

Your child may want to keep a pile of these word cards or to throw each one out. Leave it up to him. With or without the card, the child will have the experience of seeing a word that's important to him written down, carrying it around for a while, and disposing of it or keeping it at his discretion.

**Helpful Hint**

A little travel soap case is handy for carrying word cards around or storing them in a bedside table.

# 30 Hit the Library!

> *Helps develop: ability to see the library as a resource, understand the purpose of books, view reading as part of life*

*"There's a place for you
and a place for me
at your local public library."*

**Before You Begin**   Find out about your local library, what its holdings are, where things are located. Maybe you've been taking your child to the library since she was a tadpole. Maybe you're just entering the doors for the first time. Either way, you can help make it *her* place by teaching her how to use it.

**You'll Need**   a book catalog; paper or notebook; pencil; your local library; book bag

**What to Do**

1 Talk with your child about the need for a new book or two around the house. Suggest that you plan a trip to the library together.

2 Ask your child what kind of book she'd like to read. If you want, look through a mail-order book catalog for some ideas.

3 Make a list of a few specific books or topics to look for at the library.

4 Take your list and your child to the library. Plan to spend at least an hour there.

5 Use the card catalog or computer search to look up your book or topic. Guide your child through every step. Let her type her topic into the computer. Help her jot down information about where to find the book.

6 Go look for the book. Show your child how the books are ordered by number and letter. Get a librarian to demonstrate for you if needed. Have your child help search out the book she wants. Think aloud. "Let's see, the author of *Heckedy Peg* is named Wood. That starts with a *W*. Help me look through these *W*s. It's the big brown book, remember? Is it here?"

**Follow-up Activities**

- Check out your book on your library card, or, if your child is old enough, register her for a card. Note the due date and, when you get home, have your child write *library* on the due date on your calendar in invented writing.
- Supply a book bag for your child to tote library books in.
- Give yourselves a library tour. Read signs to your child. Show her copy machines, card catalogs, computer search terminals, the reference desk, the bathroom, the book drop, and so on. Ask library personnel to tell you and your child what happens in each area.

**What's Happening**

Children learn what they live. If your father's a chef, you grow up eating great food. If you mother's a musician, you grow up hearing and playing music. If your parents take you to the library and show you how it works—well, you know what the result will be. This can be a tough one for parents who didn't grow up going to the library themselves and who aren't comfortable with the procedures. If you're not sure, let your child see you find information. Demonstrate for your child how to ask questions, how to frame and solve problems, even how to read books you're not completely sure of.

**Moving Ahead**

Don't forget to take books out for yourself as well as for your child. Let your child come along while you explore the adult section of the library and search out a book. By doing so, you drive home the purposes of other areas of the building besides the children's room; you demonstrate once again the process of finding and selecting books; and you give your child the opportunity to extend you the courtesy of waiting and watching.

**Helpful Hint**

If possible, visit other libraries in other areas. Make the local library a destination on a rainy day while you're on vacation. This makes visiting libraries an exciting event—and an opportunity for comparison. What's more, it allows you to focus on the books as a familiar face in a strange place. "Look! They read *George and Martha* here too!"

# PART THREE

# The Writing Connection

How does a child best learn to write? By making writing up as she goes along. This is called *invented writing:* what comes out of the child's head and onto the paper at any age, at any level. A child starts with scribbles, moves on to drawing, then adds letters, and ultimately begins writing words. If she's reading as she learns to write, she'll apply more and more of what she picks up from books and other language activities to what she puts on paper. A child who reads will learn to write through trial and error, exploration, and practice.

Use the activities in this section as jumping-off points for encouraging your child to write, for writing with her, and for giving her experience in different kinds of writing. Remember that reading and writing go hand in hand. If you've picked up this book for help with writing, you'll want to check the other sections for ideas too. Writing flows through all language study—and through every activity in this book.

FAT CAT

# 31 Simon Says

*Simon knows everyone has played this one!*

**Before You Begin**  You probably know this game. Before you start, you have to choose someone to be Simon, the leader.

**You'll Need**  several players

**What to Do**  
1 Whoever was chosen to be Simon stands facing the players.

2 Simon gives an action command with or without the words *Simon says* before it, and demonstrates the action.

3 Players obey Simon's commands only if Simon uses the words *Simon says*. Simon has to try to trick them into copying him even when he doesn't say *Simon says*. Here's an example:

"Simon says, Put your hands on your head."

"Simon says, Wave your right hand."

"Simon says, Put your pinky finger on your knee."

"Do a somersault."

"Oops! Caught you. Everybody who did a somersault is out. Simon didn't say to do a somersault."

4 Continue playing until there's just one player left. That person becomes the next Simon.

**Follow-up Activity**  Try playing this game sitting down, while waiting in the car or at a bus stop. The movements will necessarily be smaller and more detailed: pull on your ear, raise one or two fingers, and so on. For a goofy variation, lie together on your backs on the floor and play Simon Says with foot and leg movements.

Your child is matching movements, a vital part of learning to write clearly. To copy someone's movement, you have to first notice the movement to see what the leader is doing, then direct your body to do the same thing. Simon Says requires doing this quickly. Let your child be the leader. Notice how quickly and intensely you sometimes have to think in order to replicate his movements. It's also great for your child's confidence and speaking ability to be Simon and direct you. Not only does he have to think of a movement, he has to do it and describe it to you. Simon has to be able to think on his feet too.

**Moving Ahead** Make a stack of cards with ready-made instructions for Simon. For younger children, include stick drawings with the words. This adds a new challenge for the person being Simon: he has to read, act on what he reads, and direct others to do the same. And he has to remember not to say *Simon says* sometimes too!

**Helpful Hint** Give a younger child extra practice on his own to help him get quicker at responding. Try Simon Says when your child's in the bathtub: "Simon says, Dump the cups." "Simon says, Fill the smallest cup with water." You'll be giving him extra language experiences too!

FROM
HERE TO THERE

# Get on Track

*Helps develop:*
*visual and move-*
*ment matching, analy-*
*sis of shape, designs,*
*directions, and letters*

*This activity gives you a chance to be*
*"Barney Google, with the goo-goo-googly eyes."*

**Before You Begin**
Find a moment when you're face-to-face with your child, so that she can see your eyes. This game is great for traveling time (on the train or bus, not while driving!) or waiting time. I once held the attention of three children (only one of whom was mine) in the waiting room of an eye doctor's office with this activity. If you're more self-conscious, try it at home. You might want to eliminate the first follow-up activity, pointing with your tongue, depending on your surroundings.

**You'll Need**
you and your child

**What to Do**
1 Say, "Do you know what I'm doing?" Point with your hand to something to your far left. Then shift your eyes left, and say, "I'm looking at the ——— without moving my head," mentioning the object you are looking at. Do the same with objects to your right, up, and down.

2 Wait. Your child will likely follow suit. Or you can suggest something for her to look at without moving her head.

3 Next show your child another way to use her eyes. Roll them. Say to your child, "I'm making a circle with my eyes." Invite her to follow your finger with her eyes as you move it in a circle. Ask her to make a shape with her finger for your eyes to follow.

**Follow-up Activities**
• Now do the same activities with your tongue. Ask your child, "What shapes can you make with your tongue?" Or use your tongue to point at things that are moving or standing still.

86

- Use any part of your body to draw a letter or a shape like a letter (for example, an upside-down *T*) in the air. Offer to guess what shape your child is making.

**What's Happening**

*Letter formation requires a fine imitative motion of a very small body part, the fingers, over a very small area, a space on a sheet of paper. Getting to the point of being able to form letters well with a pencil is facilitated by practice without a pencil, without the paper, but with a small and specific body part. Eyes, elbow, fingertip are all ideal.*

*One of the earliest developed aspects of letter formation is the ability to track an object from point A to point B. Babies learn to do this with their eyes, as they follow the motion of a mobile or a parent. Those eyes learn to narrow their focus through practice watching objects as they move along a path. The next step toward letter formation is to trace that path, then to create your own. The child who is able to form letters clearly has well-developed fine motor skills as well as the ability to imitate a shape by moving from point A to point B in a set direction.*

**Moving Ahead**

Use any available opportunities to encourage your child to practice tracking with her eyes and other body parts. Follow the progress of one vehicle from one end of the street to another. Play copycat, using body parts to make weird designs. Most challenging: track the path of one raindrop from the top of the window to the sill. Have a raindrop race, or just watch to see the various paths the different drops take.

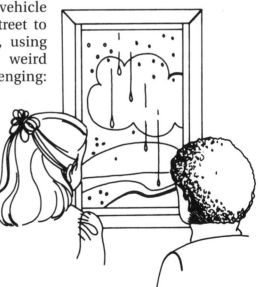

**Helpful Hint**     Here's a fun finger game to teach your child.

*Say:*                                      *Do:*

Going on a treasure hunt,
going on a treasure hunt ........ *Walk fingers up child's back*

X marks the spot .............. *Draw an X on her back*

Three big circles .............. *Draw three circles*

And a great big dot ............ *One strong poke with finger*

Going up ..................... *Walk up to neck*

Going down .................. *Walk back down back*

Going all around .............. *Move fingers in a spiral*

Dry land .................... *Rub back with palms*

Marshy land ................. *Tickle under arms*

Wind ....................... *Blow in ear*

Egg! ....................... *Thump lightly on head*

# 33 Yellow Jell-O

*Rhyme time.
Smart start?
Quite right!*

**Before You Begin**

Once your child has experience reading nursery rhymes or playing with rhymes (see Activity 26: Rhymin' Around), it's time to make something of those rhymes.

**You'll Need**

paper; crayons, markers, or paint; stapler and/or tape

**What to Do**

1 Start by saying rhymes to your child, something nonsensical that you make up, such as "I was downtown and I saw a *big pig.*"

2 Encourage your child to add to the story with his own rhymes. " . . . and I saw a *fat cat.*" Play around with the rhymes until you've said a good many together.

3 Then draw pictures of one rhyme at a time: the fat cat, the pink drink, the bug on a rug.

4 Give the pictures labels. Or make a story of them, writing the plot below the pictures. Follow your child's initiative in this. (There's bound to be a lot of giggling!)

5 Staple or tape the pictures together to form a book.

BIG PIG

**Follow-up Activities**

- Invite your child to write labels for the pictures and/or write the story in invented writing.

- Ask your child to read the finished book to you and to others.

FAT CAT

What you're working toward is an understanding that one letter can change the sound and meaning of a word, but you're doing it indirectly. The key here is that rhymes are fun, joyous. When you encourage your child to create his own poems, illustrated ones at that, by putting two rhyming words together, you bring him into the joy of joining words together for humor and fun. Think of kids who learn their first knock-knock jokes. They realize the power of words to make people laugh, groan, and tell more knock-knock jokes. Words are power!

**Moving Ahead**

Use a movable alphabet such as magnet letters or letter blocks to help your child create rhyming words. Start, for example, with the word *pan*. Take off the *p* and substitute *c*. This works best with a child who already knows some initial sounds.

**Helpful Hint**

Challenge an older child's mind by playing Hinky Pinky. You think up and ask a question whose answer is a two-word rhyme, and the child has to think of the rhyme. For example:

- What's the name for a hot drink an insect likes? (flea tea)
- Where do you look for recipes? (cookbook)
- What do you call a shaky lemon dessert? (yellow Jell-O)

YELLOW JELLO

# 34 Building Blocks

**H**elps develop: fine-motor and gross-motor movement, spatial understanding, matching, spoken expression, following and giving directions

*Your child can dream up whole worlds with blocks. In the wordless picture book* Changes, Changes *by Pat Hutchins (MacMillan), the little wooden dolls use blocks to build a fire truck when their block house catches fire. The fire hose floods the area, so the dolls rebuild their house as a boat, and sail away . . .*

**Before You Begin**
Make sure your child has plenty of time to explore her blocks. If your child could have only one plaything, I hope it would be building blocks. Virtually every activity in this book can be done with them: matching, forming letters, thumping out the rhythms in the syllables of words, dramatic play . . . Along with play constructions, you can build many skills and concepts with blocks.

**You'll Need**
building blocks of any kind

**What to Do**
1 Ask your child to play follow-the-leader with the blocks. Decide who will be the leader and who will follow.

2 Build two structures side by side: the leader places a block, and then the follower duplicates the leader's action on his or her own structure. If you're the leader, keep it simple: five blocks at the most.

3 When you're the leader, talk through what you're doing. Think aloud. Use words that specifically describe what you're doing. "I'm standing the yellow column on top of the red rectangle. Hmmm. Looks like a smokestack . . ."

**Follow-up Activity**

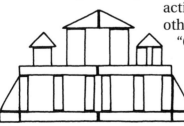

When you're the follower, think aloud as you watch your child's actions. "I see. The two blue squares are right on top of each other, with all their corners matched up." Ask questions, too. "Okay, you put a green square there. I only have a yellow square. Okay to use that?" Also, goof up. Let your child check and direct you as you correct your structure to match hers.

**Moving Ahead**

Use all sorts of different configurations with blocks when you're the leader in this game. Lay them flat, parquet style, to create a design like a checkerboard pattern or a face. Build three-dimensional buildings, people, and boats.

**Helpful Hint**

Keep your blocks in a big box or basket in the living room or another central location in your home. This keeps them accessible to visitors, babysitters, and other family members whose different building styles and vocabularies will add to your child's experience.

# 35 **Finger Play**

**H**elps develop: fine-motor movement, upper-body strength, writing

*Chances are your child will love "making her mark" by painting with water. And she'll be on the road to writing too.*

**Before You Begin**  Dress your child in old clothes, a bathing suit, or his birthday suit. This activity is best done on a warm day and must definitely be done outdoors.

**You'll Need**  surfaces for painting with water: chalkboard, sand, dirt, objects in the backyard or park; water; small bucket, can or plastic container; simple painting tool: large paintbrush, rag, sponge, stick; food coloring (optional)

**What to Do**

**1** Hand your child a bucket of water and ask him to "paint" the place with it. Suggest he use his hand, or equip him with a rag, a brush, or a stick. Or ask, "What do you think you could use for a brush?" Help him find a tool.

**2** Your child may be initially skeptical. How can you paint with water? Suggest that he try. Most things will alter in appearance when wet. If your child doesn't buy it, add food coloring to the water. (Make sure he's wearing nothing special. Food coloring can stain.)

**3** Let your child use whatever strokes and motions he wants to cover the objects he chooses. Talk to him about the motions he's making. Ask him to describe how he's covering each object.

**Follow-up Activities**

• Encourage your child to experiment with different painting tools: sponge, stick, etc.

• Expand this activity to the great indoors. Provide a chalkboard and a wet paintbrush, and suggest the child use these materials to create designs, or just cover a surface with paint.

Even the youngest child needs to "make his mark" on a surface through the weight and motion of his hand. As one art teacher I know expressed it, sweeping her arms in a circle through the air, "Kids need to go through this motion before they can wind it tighter and begin to write." Involve your child in simple activities like this one, and you help lay the foundation for the writing ahead.

This activity is not only for the very young but for any who need help developing the movements and muscles of writing. Given the right tools and the chance to experiment, children will develop the strength and control they need to write well.

**Moving Ahead**

Make available large crayons and big sheets of paper, or chalk and a sidewalk. Anything goes!

**Helpful Hint**

All children need plenty of practice forming designs and following movements with their hands and upper bodies. See Activity 36: Designs by Hand, and Activity 37: Spring Training for Penmanship.

# 36 Designs by Hand

**H**elps develop: *movement matching, letter formation, visual memory, movement memory*

*Mud, sand, pencil, hand. Help your child see that they're all tools for writing!*

**Before You Begin**

Start pointing out designs that you find in the world. One family I know whose name starts with *Y* has a collection of tree branches in a *Y* shape. Look for designs and patterns that involve letters. They're out there!

**You'll Need**

a surface for drawing; a tool for drawing with. The surface can be anything: the mud in the backyard, the sand in the park, a tray full of cornmeal, or a sheet of paper. The tool can be a stick, a finger, a pencil, a fork, or a drinking straw.

**What to Do**

1 Start by sitting together, etching figures in wet sand, or whatever your surface is, with your finger, or whatever your tool is.

2 Observe your child's handiwork and encourage her to notice yours. Talk about what you're doing or what you see her doing. "I'm making a big spiral, like that snail shell over there," or "I see you're making a long row of *X*s."

3 Play follow-the-leader. Take turns leading and following.

4 With a very young child, make circles. Straight lines, crosses, and diagonals are harder to make. You don't have to make letters. Weird designs can be the most fun of all, and a child can create or copy even elaborate ones.

5 Talk to your child about your designs and ask her about hers. Use words like *cross, curve, straight, diagonal, over,* and *under* to talk about the movements you're making as well as the shapes that are the end product.

Look for letter shapes everywhere; in tree branches, fabric patterns, fences, and architecture: "See how the telephone poles are *T*s?"

**What's Happening**

*Children the world over sit and make designs in mud and sand, and even on paper. By taking that natural action and talking about it, you put words to what your child is doing. By playing follow-the-leader, you help develop your child's eye for the differences and similarities between designs, as well as her ability to replicate them with her own hands. Dabbling is so important to learning—nothing beats experience and play. So let your child call the shots with this one, but help her find words to name what she does.*

**Moving Ahead** Over time, play this game with different surfaces and tools. There's a natural growth from this activity into forming letters, writing words, and writing each other notes in the sand. See Activity 46: Making Letters.

**Helpful Hint** There are possibilities everywhere: steam on windows, bubbles on the bathroom wall, sponges on the kitchen counter (cut up one sponge into small pieces), cheese on a cracker, a flashlight shining on the ceiling . . .

# 37 Spring Training for Penmanship

*This builds your child's writing skills, and it gets the bathroom clean at the same time! Maybe this activity should be called "Spring Cleaning."*

**Before You Begin**  Strip your child down to underwear, or have him don a bathing suit, smock, or old clothes for this one—it can be messy.

**You'll Need**  bucket; sponge; toothpaste; old toothbrush; old cleanser container filled with baking soda; spray bottle full of one part vinegar and three parts water

**What to Do**

1 Suggest to your child, "Let's clean the bathroom!"

2 Give him the tools and some clear instruction. Don't give him any cleansers that contain harsh chemicals or fumes— just the baking soda "cleanser." Put him to work cleaning, and join in. Show him how to scrub the sink, wall, tiles, or floors. Three shakes of cleanser on a damp sponge should be plenty.

3 Play with patterns together as you scrub. Scrub in circles, waves, up, down, across, and around. Play follow-the-leader, taking turns leading.

4 Now rinse. Demonstrate how to wet the sponge in the bucket and squeeze. Wipe with one top-to-bottom stroke. Ask your child to predict how many rinses it will take to get the cleanser off.

**Follow-up Activities**
- Have your child help you clean bathtub grout with an old toothbrush and toothpaste (they get stains off grout as well as off teeth).
- Show him how to use vinegar and water (a nontoxic combination) to clean mirrors and windows.

**What's Happening**

*Baseball players don't hit the diamond the first day of the season without building up the muscles that have gone flabby over the winter. Likewise, kids don't just pick up a pen and start printing without the strength and control to form letters. Watch a young child with a pencil: his entire body moves. As a child cleans—pressing, scrubbing, moving—his arm creates up-down strokes and circles, he tones his upper body, and he is, in effect, forming the shapes that make letters. A sponge is great because it allows a child to use his hands. Toothbrushes and spray bottles require even greater control.*

**Moving Ahead**

Take your cleaning equipment elsewhere: go outside and wash the car or your child's bicycle; scrub the kitchen floor; wash and wipe windows or dishes. Show your child how to use the various cleaners and tools used to perform these tasks. Involve him in dusting, vacuuming, bed making, laundry folding. Show him the steps and the materials involved in each process and encourage his mastery of them. He'll develop proficiency, confidence, and all the good eye-hand perceptual skills listed above.

**Helpful Hint**

Add a few speckles of green powdered cleanser to the baking soda to add authenticity. A drop or two of blue food coloring makes the vinegar water more fun too.

# 38 Real-Life Stories

*Your child will love hearing a story about you "once upon a time."*

**Before You Begin**  Think up something that happened to you when you were young that you'd like to share with your child.

**You'll Need**  a few memories of yourself as a child; photo albums, diaries, recordings of your voice as a child (optional)

**What to Do**  
**1** Simply ask, "Do you want to hear a story?"

**2** Tell about what happened to you. You don't have to go on very long, tell it fabulously, or include exciting twists of plot. If it's a story about something that happened to you, it's bound to have fascination for your child.

**3** Pause to talk about how you felt at pivotal moments in the story.

**4** Tell the same story twice or more. Alter it a little. Point out your changes to your child if she doesn't pick up on them herself. "Did you notice I added that the doll's hair was black this time? I felt that was important today," or "This time I said that the kids actually touched the dead shark. I remembered that that's what made it so exciting."

**Follow-up Activity**  Talk about people in the story whom your child knows now. Describe what they were like back then. Pull out a photo album and show your child. Or read a diary entry that tells about the event in the story.

**What's Happening**

*Make your past real to your child, and you make another period in history real, helping her to develop a sense of chronology as well as empathy for the whole person you are. Tell stories about yourself and you encourage your child to tell her own stories about herself, to follow your example in dramatizing and describing feelings and events, to express herself (literally!) through language. What's more, when you change your story to make it better, you model the process of revision for your child.*

**Moving Ahead**

Develop a repertoire of stories about your childhood. Offer them to your child when you're in the car or on the bus. If you like, ask her to help you write them down and illustrate them.

**Helpful Hint**

Use a few old pictures to make a photo album of you as a child, for your child. Together, write captions for the pictures, talk about what happened, where, when, and to whom.

# 39 Drawing Out a Story

**H**elps develop:
composing,
revising, writing

*Ask your child, "What's the story of this picture?"*

**Before You Begin**  Take a look at a drawing your child has just finished. Encourage him to talk about it.

**You'll Need**  your child and a drawing he has put a lot of heart into

**What to Do**

1  Ask, "What's the story of this picture?" His response will be a story, or at least, "There's no story. It's just a picture of a rainbow." Then, you can say, "Why's the rainbow there?" Get into nonfiction: "What colors are in a rainbow? Where do they come from?" The story of a picture doesn't have to be a story, per se; it can be factual.

2  Listen raptly. Ask further questions in a conversational manner. "I thought you said the elephant is looking for peanuts. Where are the peanuts?" The child may reach for a crayon to add them or may have a good reason that there aren't any peanuts in the picture—another aspect of the story.

3  Use the drawing and the story behind it as the springboard for writing. Some options:

   • "Will you tell the story again so I can save it on the tape recorder?"

   • "Will you tell the story again so I can write it down?"

   • "Will you write the story down to help me remember it?"

4  Once it's written or recorded, ask him to read the story (or play the recording of it) to you and others.

**Follow-up Activity**  Talk about changes your child made in his story when he told it the second time around. "This time the elephant found peanuts. How come?"

**What's Happening**  *Drawing is the beginning of writing. Your child is discovering what it means to take an idea or image and flesh it out as a story with beginning, middle, and end. When you talk to your child about his story, you're having a writers' conference, discussing the elements that work together to make a story. When you help your child find a way of keeping his story, through recording, dictation, or invented writing, you emphasize the ways of saving language. Encourage your child to share his story, to put it away, to change it over and over: it's his. And don't neglect to point out all those books in the library just full of other people's recorded stories. Now your child is an author too!*

**Moving Ahead**  Don't hesitate to use computer drawing and word processing programs to have your child create stories. Just as adults can drive without understanding car engines, children can write without understanding spelling, mechanics, or letter formation—and their drawings show that they're ready to write stories at a young age.

**Helpful Hint**  Here's what *not* to do when talking to a child about a drawing. Don't ask, "What's this?" You might get a string of description, but no plot: "It's a rainbow with a butterfly and a bear." Don't guess, "I know. It's an elephant!" Think about the kinds of answers you might get to that gambit. A nod? A blank stare? A furious *no*? Ask for the *story*.

# 40 Talk Like a Robot

**H**elps develop: speaking, dramatic play, an ear for tone and cadence, patterns of language and conversation

*Writing is talk written down. There are as many different ways of talking as there are people. Get your child to listen. Try various styles of talking. Flexibility with spoken language makes your child a better writer.*

**Before You Begin** Listen to voices. With the television on, close your eyes and try to identify people by their voices. Listen to people talking in another room, in a restaurant, on the radio, on a tape recording of the family. Who's who? How do their voices differ?

**You'll Need** your voice and your child's

**What to Do**

1 Ask your child, "Whose voice can you do? Daddy's? Barney's? The witch from *The Wizard of Oz*? A robot's?"

2 Demonstrate your robot voice. "Danger, Will Robinson! . . . R2, where are you? . . . *beep* . . . *zoop* . . . That does not compute!"

3 Have a conversation with your child in robot talk. Both be robots. Or be a robot parent and a robot child.

4 Talk about the things you see from the car, bus, or train in robot talk. Create movements to match.

**Follow-up Activity** Now try other voices. Talk like a dog, a baby, a prince, a newscaster, a country singer.

**What's Happening** *Dramatic play is an important precursor to writing. Having fun with your child creating new voices and dialogues together is a way of focusing dramatic play on language. It'll also teach your child to focus his ear on the different ways in which people speak. How you respond to different voices, accents, and attitudes can be an education in itself for your child. You can use your response to broaden your child's horizons, to demonstrate your acceptance of many different people and their ways of speaking. It's important to always be respectful of the way people speak, of course. Through listening and imitating, you help your child tune in to oral language and to become more flexible about language.*

**Moving Ahead** As your child grows in understanding, share new ways of expressing language: American Sign Language, Braille, Morse Code, even pig Latin, and written codes. Each of these will strengthen your child's fluency in language and his understanding of how it is constructed and used.

**Helpful Hint** Here's a simple talking exercise. Choose one word—for example, your name. Have your child say it many different ways: loudly, softly, happily, sadly, as if he were sick, tired, hungry, whiny, joyful.

# 41 Sign Me Up

*"Show me your muscle!" demands the five-year-old.
I flex. She reaches out to touch my elbow.
"That's not my muscle!" I say.
What we need here is labels!*

**Before You Begin**   Use your parental intuition to figure out something your child doesn't have all the names for. Parts of an arm? Parts of a telephone?

**You'll Need**   masking tape; small pieces of paper *or* Post-it self-stick notes; pencil

**What to Do**

1 Decide on a set of things to name for your child: pieces of clothing, parts of a room, the bath toys, your body.

2 Give the child the masking tape and paper. You keep the pencil.

3 Start by identifying one of the items. For example, say, "Okay, this is my elbow."

4 Write a label saying *elbow*, or have your child write it in invented writing. (The point here is vocabulary, not spelling.)

5 Have your child attach the label to the appropriate object and read it back to you.

6 Continue until you've labeled ten or so objects. Read them through again with your child.

**Follow-up Activity**   Not sure what something is called? Consult an expert (or a book written by an expert). Show your child how to use a diagram in a book (the car manual is ideal), something with labels connected to the parts of an

105

object, just as they're now connected to parts of you, your house, your dog (if it's the complacent kind), your clothes closet . . . If you can't find a correct technical word, make up a name for the object in question with your child.

**What's Happening**

*Writing is a way to remember. For a child, labeling things with their names is an extension of the baby game (a vitally important one) of pointing at objects and asking, "Dat?" The parent names the object, and the baby takes a giant step forward in language acquisition. It's the same with writing. Let your child know that everything has a name that can be written and stuck on, and you'll help her develop a rich vocabulary. What's more, by finding—with your child— the correct names for things, you help her to draw conclusions about the purpose and function of objects. Your dishwasher has a* latch. *So does the car door. So does her lunch box. They're different-looking things, but they all play the same role of keeping things shut.*

**Moving Ahead**

Visit a shop tended by a knowledgeable person. My favorite is Uncle Sam's Umbrella Shop in New York. The owner knows the name of every part of an umbrella, and I was fascinated to hear them. Did you and your child know that an umbrella has spokes, a spine, a handle, a crook? Ask questions with your child—and go home and label your umbrella.

**Helpful Hint**

If you use masking tape, don't leave it on longer than a week or so. Beyond that, it might leave a sticky residue.

# 42 The New Version

*H*elps develop: *storytelling, speaking, identification of attributes of a story, writing*

*What if the Fourth Little Pig built a house like Frank Lloyd Wright's, with a river running through it, and the Big Bad Wolf swam right in? Your child's imagination is the best learning tool available.*

**Before You Begin**   Read a story with your child, or, if possible, several versions of the same story. (See references in the Helpful Hints at the end of this activity.)

**You'll Need**   simple story books; several versions of or sequels to fairy tales (optional); pencil and paper

**What to Do**   

1 Suggest that your child help you think of a story about something else that could happen to the characters in this story. What did Goldilocks do the day after she visited the three bears? What kind of house did the Fourth Little Pig build? You don't like the scary parts of *Rapunzel*? Let's change them.

2 Let your child spin the yarn of his own choosing, based on the characters in the book and the new events he makes up.

3 Involve other people in the story (for example, other family members in the car). Keep each other going: "What happened after that?" Encourage everyone to be flexible about the route the story takes.

**Follow-up Activity**   Work together to write or record your story. If you write it, have your child help you illustrate it. Dress up stuffed animals or puppets as the characters and photograph them, or draw pictures to illustrate. If you record it, rehearse the voices of the different characters. Rerecord until you're happy with the results. Share the story with others.

**What's Happening**

*F*lexibility is a key factor in the ability to solve problems in writing as in other areas. When you open your child's mind to new ways of doing things, you encourage the child to see that there are multiple interpretations of any situation. Children can easily get locked into one version of things, insisting that a game be played a certain way or that a story can only have one plot. It's important for children to be able to switch, to think of things from a new standpoint, and to work within new structures. The goal of the adult is to understand as much as possible of the child's interpretation, to ask open-ended questions, to encourage self-expression, and to gently lead the way down new paths.

**Moving Ahead**

Tell your school-aged child the parable of the blind men and the elephant. Each man described the elephant differently depending on the part of the animal he touched: tusks, tail, trunk, leg, side, ear. Help your child to see that what's true for one person isn't always true for others, and that life has room for many perspectives.

**Helpful Hint**

There are many books available to help you with this story activity.

- Your library has books with pick-your-path plots to read aloud to your child. Many computer programs for children involve pick-your-path plots as well.
- Search out different versions of the same tale. For *Cinderella,* for example, try

  *Cinderella* by William Wegman (Hyperion)

  *Queen of the May* by Steven Kroll (Holiday House)

  *The Korean Cinderella* by Shirley Climo (HarperCollins)

# 43 The Family Notebook

*Writing becomes a tool for you and your family to use to communicate information, advice, requests, encouragement, love—all in one little notebook.*

**Before You Begin**  Tie a string to the notebook. Tape the other end of the string to a counter top. Tie the pen to a string and thread the other end of the string through the notebook's spiral or hole.

**You'll Need**  spiral notebook; pen; string

**What to Do**

1 Tell your family, "There are a lot of things we need to tell each other. Let's use this notebook to write everything down."

2 Don't make rules—place no restrictions on what people should write. And don't insist on writing alone—pictures are welcome, too. Emphasize that this is a place to share thoughts with the family.

3 Encourage your child to write in the notebook in invented writing. Ask her to read you what she's written. (Say, "I can't read six-year-old writing. Can you read it for me? Then I'll read you the grown-up writing here.")

**Follow-up Activities**

- Use the notebook yourself to model different forms of communication for your child:

  to write an encouraging note

  to draw a picture or comic strip

  to ask someone to do a chore (or remind someone of a forgotten chore)

  to claim the TV for a certain time

to make an announcement

to establish a rule

to apologize

- Read the notebook with your child. Talk about the different writing levels and styles of family members.
- Encourage house guests or other visitors to make entries in the notebook. Talk about their writing patterns with your child.

**What's Happening**  *The most important purpose of writing is self-expression. Who better to express yourself to than your family? Your child learned to talk in the family environment; this activity allows you to teach her writing in a similar way. Just as she learned to understand the different tones, levels, and vocabulary of different family members' speech, she will learn different styles of writing, handwriting, and usage of writing. Through this activity, writing becomes social. In order to communicate, your child must use reading and writing.*

**Moving Ahead**  When you fill up one notebook, buy another. Keep the old one on hand. Your child can reread it to find out what was happening in the family when the notebook was written. She'll also note growth and changes in her own ability to write—a sign that her writing continues to progress.

**Helpful Hint**  Too busy to write in a notebook? Have your child take dictation for you, in invented writing, then read it back to you and other family members.

# 44 Pictures of Things

*Your child can look at just so many books about other places and things before she needs to create a real-life book of her own.*

**Before You Begin**    Read some non-fiction books with your child. Your library has many picture books that are photo essays—photographs with accompanying description and commentary. Check the geography and travel sections, and look for picture books by Tana Hoban and Bruce McMillan.

**You'll Need**    camera; film; album—ready-made is okay, but handmade is more personal and flexible; pencils, crayons, paste, or stick-on corners to hold photographs

**What to Do**    1  Take your child for a walk around your neighborhood and photograph key scenes: buildings, people, intersections, doors, dogs, cows, whatever strikes your child's fancy. If your camera is relatively simple, your child can be the photographer. Or ask him to be the model, standing with or in front of the subjects.

2  Get your pictures developed. Put them in your album, using them as the illustrations for a book about your neighborhood.

3  Have your child write (in invented writing) or dictate to you labels or a story for the pictures. It's up to the child to decide if there should be a story or just explanation in the captions. Add these to the album.

4  Create a cover and dream up a title for the book.

**Follow-up Activity**   Carry the book with you on another walk around the neighborhood. Locate the spots featured in the book. This is an especially effective thing to do with another child or adult who hasn't seen the book before. Have your child read his book to this audience and encourage the newcomer to seek out the landmarks pictured.

**What's Happening**   *Real people write books about their lives. This becomes apparent to a child when you have him write his own book about an aspect of his life. Talk about the choices people make as to what they include in their books and photographs. Through making the translation of real life into book form, a child learns the purpose and function of nonfiction writing. Through looking at examples of nonfiction books and writing his own, a child comes to understand the process of reporting and can extend that understanding to the use of nonfiction books in research.*

**Moving Ahead**   Use your book to help your child make comparisons between your neighborhood and other areas. Find books about other cities or localities. Talk with your child about the similarities and differences and use your findings to trigger discussions about how other people do things: build buildings, set up playgrounds, decorate houses, and so on.

**Helpful Hints**
- Children who travel with their parents are sometimes asked by teachers to keep journals of their trip. Help your child to recall, describe, and explain by creating a photo journal with him. Compare this book with the one you made of your home territory.
- A child who spends time in two different homes will especially benefit from this activity. He can take his neighborhood along wherever he goes—especially if he makes two books.

# 45 Tape Tech

**H**elps develop: speaking, cause and effect, use of a machine, process of making a tape recording, process of writing

*Hear me roar!*

**Before You Begin**    Share some audio book kits with your child. Let her see how they work: you listen to the story while following along in the book. When the beep sounds, you turn the page. Also, familiarize your child with the workings of the tape recorder. Make sure he knows how to operate the buttons to record, to play, and to stop.

**You'll Need**    portable tape player with microphone; cassettes; batteries; paper and pencil

**What to Do**    1 Let your child experiment with recording and playing back his voice on the tape recorder.

2 Ask him to record something for you to listen to. Enjoy it with him and talk about it. "What's that interesting sound?" "That joke was funny." "You were talking about something you saw out the window of the car—what was it?"

3 Pick up on something that is part of your child's recording. Encourage him to expand the idea into a larger recording. Here are some ideas:

- a story
- a running commentary or guide to a route you travel in the car
- an explanation or description of how something works or happens

**Follow-up Activity**    Ask your child to illustrate his recording. He may wish to make one drawing or a few to go with beeps he makes on the recording. Let him decide how much to do. Listen to the recording with your child and study the drawing for the points he mentions in the recording. Talk to him about his work and the words he used to express his ideas. Suggest that he write the words to go with his drawing, using invented writing.

**What's Happening**    Spoken language is transitory: say something and it's gone. Words are formed as you speak and are lost just as quickly. Writing is one way of saving language, but it requires an intermediary: the hand. Taping speech is one of the simplest ways that a young child learns that language can be saved, recalled over and over, changed, and saved again. When a child tapes his words, he's writing. When he listens to a tape of his words, he's essentially reading something he's written. When he talks with you about what he wants to change, he's having an editorial meeting. And when he retapes and changes his sounds or story, he's making a revision.

When a child uses a tape recorder, he learns to use a machine. It's good development of his understanding of technology and forms a foundation for seeing a story in linear fashion. He'll gain a wealth of knowledge about the working of machines, the creation of a product (his tape), and the control of a medium that allows him to record, save, and change his own writing.

**Moving Ahead**    Let a child create a tape and drawing or book for a friend. Let an older child create a set for a younger child.

**Helpful Hint**    Rechargeable batteries are a must!

# PART FOUR

# Language Ins and Outs

This section deals with the grammar and mechanics of writing in more detail. The activities in this section provide opportunities for you to underline important concepts for your child and to increase her reading, writing, and speaking vocabulary, making experience and exploration the teachers. You'll find activities for helping your child form letters, connect letters with the sounds they make, figure out syllables, and understand the purpose of punctuation. Clearly, children at different levels of reading and writing will need different activities. Find the ones that work for your child.

These activities are fun language games, not the keys to reading and writing. Your child will pick up many, many concepts through reading with you and to you. These activities will add to your child's expertise and enjoyment of language, provided you have the ability to say brightly, "Hey, that's an interesting answer. Try this one."

Let me caution you. With quantifiable, right-and-wrong topics like these, it's easy to fall into testing your child, using words like *right* and *wrong* and making comparisons between your child and others. *DON'T.* Instead, just play the games. Then if you feel an urge to "do" more language, pick up a book. Go snuggle on the couch with your child, and read something in a cozy, accepting atmosphere.

# 46 Making Letters

**H**elps develop:
*letter formation,
fine-motor skills, tac-
tile and visual memory*

*How does E feel?
How do you make an R?
Can you bake—and eat—a Z?*

**Before You Begin**  Make sure your child can recognize some letters before you try this activity. You'll find other letter forming and identification activities in the other sections. This activity is included in this section because its focus is how letters are formed, put together, rather than how they are used to form words. Some children will get this almost through osmosis as they read and practice writing. Others need the boost that touching, manipulating, and even tasting provide. Use Activity 36: Designs by Hand as a follow-up.

**You'll Need**  movable letters; sandpaper; scissors; clay or dough for modeling *or* cookie dough for eating

**What to Do**

1 Have your child choose a letter from his name and find it from his pile of movable letters.

2 Ask your child to use a finger to trace the letter.

3 Tell your child that you're going to make the letter out of sandpaper. Ask her to direct you as you draw or trace the letter on the sandpaper.

4 Help your child cut out the sandpaper letter.

5 Repeat this process until you have all the letters of your child's name.

6 Let your child play with the letters, arranging them, rearranging them, placing them in piles, rubbing her fingers over the sandpaper, or doing whatever else she wants with them.

**Follow-up Activity**    Suggest that your child use the letters as a guide to make the letters in her name out of clay or cookie dough. Finish up: if you used clay, let it harden, and paint it. If dough, bake it and then either paint it or eat it.

---

**What's Happening**    The more senses involved in perceiving something, the better it will be understood, replicated, and recalled. Through this activity, you involve your child in touching letters, moving them around, talking about them, comparing them visually, and constructing them.

Your child is already immersed in letters if you are reading to her, talking to her about signs, mail, television, and other media in which writing appears. She becomes involved with writing as she makes the letters her own through exploring them, tracing, coloring, and constructing them with a variety of materials.

---

**Moving Ahead**    Use letters made from sandpaper, clay, or dough as templates for tracing onto paper. Doing this helps the child move from three-dimensional understanding of writing to two-dimensional understanding.

**Helpful Hint**    Try this recipe for modeling dough. It makes a big pile!

Combine:    5 cups flour

4 cups boiling water

1 cup salt

3 tablespoons alum (found in baking ingredients section of grocery)

2 tablespoons oil

food coloring (optional)

Stir until smooth. Allow to cool before using. Store in covered plastic container.

47 **Alphabet Game**

*I went to the supermarket and I bought
apples, bananas, cucumbers, and doughnuts!*

**Before You Begin**  Play this game when your child understands the initial sound concept (that a word starts with a sound and that a letter or two stands for that sound).

**You'll Need**  space for talk and/or travel

**What to Do**

1 Start with a basic category: supermarket purchases, names of people we know, names of places, things you own, nonsense words.

2 Go through the alphabet with your child, thinking of a word in your category that starts with each letter. "*A* is for *albatross.*"

3 Take turns. "*B* is for *blue jay.*"

4 Don't be rigid about spelling. Suppose your child says, "*K* is for *cuckoo.*" Just respond, "Yes! *Cuckoo* does start with a *K* sound." For an older child with reading and writing experience, you can add, "But you know the *K* sound can be made by *K* or *C* or *Q*. Which do you think makes the first sound in *cuckoo*?"

5 Don't insist on real words either. One family I know has given up on finding words in every category for the letter *U*, partly because they all love shouting, "Ugga mugga underwear!" for *U* every time they go through the alphabet. The point is to learn sounds, and sometimes that's better accomplished with nonsense than with real words.

**Follow-up Activity**     On each turn, repeat all that has come before, adding the next letter and a new word. You can also give answers within a sentence that adds to the meaning. "I packed my grandmother's trunk, and in it I packed ambrosia, boots, carpet cleaner . . ." Or, "Guess what followed me home! An anteater, a brontosaurus, a camera man . . ."

**What's Happening**     Your child is learning to think of the alphabet sequentially, at the same time that he's learning the sounds the letters make at the beginning of the words, at the same that he's thinking of words that start with the right letter and that fit the category of names that you're working on, at the same time that he's exercising his memory, at the same time that he's learning new words—and of course you'll want to stop and explain what a llama is, what a mongoose is, what kind of a name Niobe is—at the same time that he's having a good time talking it up with a parent. Whew!

**Moving Ahead**     With your child, explore a picture dictionary. Note the different kinds of objects that start with the letter *A*, the letter *B*, and so on. Consider making your own picture dictionary in a notebook. Or create a set of alphabet cards on unlined index cards with pictures and names.

**Helpful Hint**     See Activity 5: From Alpha to Omega for ways to use alphabet books to add to the fun of this activity.

# 48 **Wordy Workout**

**H**elps develop:
*speaking, initial
consonants, listening,
memory, mouth muscles*

*Swan swims over the sea. Swim, swan, swim!
Swan swam back again. Well swum, swan!*

**Before You Begin**    Try this with several children. Tongue twisters are a great leveler: kids of different ages and abilities can handle them equally well and can often do better than adults.

**You'll Need**    tongue-twister poems (included in many nursery rhyme books)

**What to Do**    **1** Recite a tongue twister for your child and encourage her to try it out.
Some simple (but tricky) ones:
- Unique New York *(repeat)*
- The big black bug bled big black blood. *(repeat)*
- Rubber baby buggy bumpers *(repeat)*

**2** Talk about what makes these tongue twisters so hard to say. Help your child point out sounds that are often repeated or sounds that are difficult to pronounce back-to-back or simply confusing sounds.

**3** Encourage your child to think up her own tongue twisters. There's no need to mention that most start with the same letter or sound. This idea will come naturally in time, and meanwhile she'll have fun playing with words just for the sound of them.

**Follow-up Activity**    Encourage your child to collect tongue-twisters by asking friends which ones they know.

*Like rhyming, tongue twisters and alliteration are ways to focus on similar sounds and spellings in words. They're fun and challenging and good for developing enunciation. More food for thought: research shows that children who eat a lot of mushy foods and not enough crunchy or chewy foods have difficulty with enunciation. Make sure that your child's diet includes foods that have some crunch to them: carrots, apples, pretzels, cucumbers, and so on.*

**Moving Ahead**

Read your child tongue twisters, moving your finger along under the words. If your child already knows many initial sounds, you might point out that many of the words share sounds and letters.

**Helpful Hint**

Dr. Seuss's *Oh Say Can You Say?* (Random House) is a great source of tongue twisters. Or try these tongue twisters:

- How much wood would a woodchuck chuck if a woodchuck could chuck wood?
- Twin-screw steel cruiser (included in Webster's definition of *tongue twister*)
- A dead rose, a live rose, a dead rose, a live rose . . . *(repeat)*

**49** # New Directions

> **H**elps develop:
> *fine-motor move-*
> *ment, following direc-*
> *tions, giving directions,*
> *vocabulary, spatial*
> *understanding*

*Over, under, around, through, up, down . . .*

**Before You Begin**

Measure and mark rows of dots about 1½ inches (4 cm) apart on the plywood. Have your child hammer nails into the dots, leaving ½ to 1 inch (1.3 to 2.5 cm) standing above the surface. Give your child the rubber bands and let him figure out how to stretch them across the nails on the nail board. Make another nail board with him or do it yourself while he explores the first one. (If you want, paint the board.)

**You'll Need**

two 8-by-18-inch (20-by-46-cm) squares of plywood, with edges sanded; 1½-inch (4-cm) nails; small hammer; rubber bands of various colors, widths, and sizes; paint (optional)

**What to Do**

**1** Watch as your child makes designs on his nail board with rubber bands. Ask, "Can you show me how to make that design on my board?"

**2** Follow your child's lead as he demonstrates either through actions or words. If he's not sure how to direct you, take a close look at his design and think aloud as you replicate it. "Let's see, first here's a long brown one across three nails. Then . . ."

**3** Make a simple design on your board for your child to follow. Always think aloud, describing your actions.

**Follow-up Activities**

- Make more complex designs, layering rubber bands in different directions.
- Take turns playing follow-the-leader.

122

- Use precise vocabulary to describe placement, direction, color, and so on. "I'm placing a blue one vertically on the first two nails in the left-hand column." Don't worry about using vocabulary that's over your child's head, because he'll get your meaning by watching your actions. Try to include the following words:

  *straight, under, parallel, around, over, across, diagonal, perpendicular, zigzag, horizontal, vertical, column*

**What's Happening**  *The transition from three-dimensional to two-dimensional representation is difficult for a child. Speaking can be the bridge. If your child can describe an action or design in words, then he'll be able to draw it, and later to write a description of it. You can build confidence in this area with this activity, as you increase your child's finger strength and understanding of how space is covered by lines and shapes (preliminary to writing).*

**Moving Ahead**  Make a diagram of the game by drawing a square with dots inside to represent the nails on the nail board. Make copies of the diagram, and have your child transfer his favorite designs to the diagrams. Staple them together to make a booklet of ideas for other players.

**Helpful Hint**  This game makes a great homemade gift from your child to a friend.

# 50 Big Words

**H**elps develop: categorization, vocabulary

*The world is full of words—many are new to your child, and some may be to you too. Explore the world of words together.*

**Before You Begin**   Talk to your child about a store she would like to visit and learn more about. Tell her that you're going to go on a word search there.

**You'll Need**   notebook; pencil

**What to Do**

**1** Bringing along the notebook and pencil, arrive at the store. Tell your child, "Okay, we're on the lookout for words here." Tell her that she'll be the word finder. You'll be the scribe and write down in the notebook the words she finds.

**2** Between you, decide on a signal for your child to give you when she hears or reads a word she likes.

**3** Explore the store. Here are some ways to gather words to write down:

- Read the labels on the aisles. Talk about the categories they describe. For example, if you're in a record store, you might see Rock 'n' Roll, Jazz, Blues, Classical, Zydeco, Broadway, Disco, Hip Hop, . . .

- Ask a store clerk for help. If you're in the lumber store, ask the clerk to describe the types of woods you can buy there: oak, plywood, pine, maple, chipboard . . .

- Read a list that's posted. For example, a list of breads in a bakery might include: pumpernickel, rye, sourdough, French, Italian, whole wheat, white . . .

- Read packages. If you're in a toy store, for example, read the names of games: Monopoly, Sorry!, Ker-Plunk, Go to the Head of the Class, Hungry Hungry Hippos . . .

**4** Back home, read your words to each other. Talk about how they look on the page, how they sound, and how things might have gotten their names. Discuss with your child why she wanted each word written down. What about it appealed to her?

**5** Together think of a title for your list of words, something that describes what they're about.

**Follow-up Activity**   Try to find out what the names mean. Study the game boxes to figure out what each interestingly named game has inside, listen to the music playing in the record store and ask someone what category it falls into, identify the breads by the labels on their bins.

---

***What's Happening***   The message? Words are pleasure. Words are fascinating. Words have meanings that can be determined by context, by asking questions, by taking a closer look. Words can be possessed by writing them down. Each place has its own words. Most of all, words stand for things that really exist.

---

**Moving Ahead**   Keep your list in your notebook. Visit other places and gather more word lists. Think of new places to go to find words, and write their names on the top of a page. Then go looking for the words: subway words, restaurant words, hardware store words, and so on.

**Helpful Hint**   Not sure what something's called? Encourage your child to make up her own word for it.

# 51 Word Study

Helps develop: word analysis, vocabulary, concept of syllables

*Did you ever see a butter fly?*
*Did you ever see a board walk?*

**Before You Begin**   Talk with your child about the way words are formed of parts. Begin with compound words, words made up of two words: *basketball, toothache, chalkboard.* Who thought up these words, you might ask your child, and why?

**You'll Need**   index cards; pen or pencil; scissors

**What to Do**
1 Work with your child to create a list of compound words.
2 Write the words on index cards.

3 Read the words with your child. Talk with him about how these compound words came to be. How are the two meanings of *pig* and *tail*, for example, different from the meaning of *pigtail*?
4 Then have your child cut the cards so that there's a word on each half.
5 Mix up the card halves. With your child, recombine them in new, sometimes silly, ways.

**Follow-up Activity**   As you talk with your child, point out compound words. Spot them as you go around town: "Hey, look! There's a *mailbox!*" Help your child hear the words first, then begin to point them out on signs. "Look. It says *truckstop.* I wonder where they got that word?"

**What's Happening**

"What are you doing, Mom?" the three-year-old asked. The mother was sitting on the floor, finishing a quilt. Instead of quilting, she was using a needle to poke a length of yarn through the quilt and tying it into a knot on the other side. "I can show you what I'm doing and tell you why," she answered. "But I have to admit I don't know what it's called." The child watched, asked a few questions, tied a few hard-to-reach knots for his mother. "I know," he said. "We'll call them wallybundles." In that house, quilts are tied with wallybundles to this day.

Who writes the book of words, after all? Entire committees at the publishing houses that produce dictionaries are devoted to deciding which new words to include in every edition. And there are always plenty to choose from—words invented by people. It's great for children to understand that ours is an evolving language and to be encouraged to understand words, analyze them, and create their own—whether they end up in Webster's or not.

**Moving Ahead**

Think up your own compound words from two words that seem to go together: *treeleaf? childnoise?* And talk about words that go together but aren't compounds, and why not: *bus stop, flush handle, elephant ears.*

**Helpful Hint**

Here's a list of compound words to help this activity along:

*moonlight, baseball, windshield, sunflower, sunshine, football, downpour, cowboy, playground, lampshade, overall, lighthouse, swingset, toenail, keyboard, earring.*

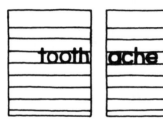

127

# 52 Syllable Synthesis

**H**elps develop:
*syllable savvy*

*Help your child think of a word as a jigsaw puzzle
made out of sounds. The sounds are the pieces.
Put them all together, and what do they make?*

**Before You Begin**   Find a quiet spot. This activity works best one-on-one, without distractions.

**You'll Need**   you and your child

**What to Do**

1 Start with your child's name. Tell her, "I'm going to say a word very slowly. It's one of my favorite words. Here are the parts of it: *E – liz – a – beth*. What do you think they make, when you put them all together?"

2 Listen to the answer. Then try another word: something shorter, not a name.

3 Ask your child to give you *her* favorite name this way.

4 Take turns saying the syllables of words and making each other guess the full word. Keep it funny and light. You're just playing with words.

**Follow-up Activity**   Try singing your child's name, giving a different note to every syllable. Encourage your child to have a fun, dramatic time singing various words with you and coming up with new word tunes on her own.

**What's Happening**    This activity will help your child begin to understand that words are divided into groups of sounds called syllables. It's easier for most children to synthesize a word—to put syllables together to make a word—than it is for them to segment it, to take it apart. The Moving Ahead activity can be a bridge between putting words together and taking them apart, because you give the word and the syllables, then ask your child to confirm whether the syllable is part of the word as she hears it. If your child is completely flummoxed by the Moving Ahead activity, she needs to go back to putting words together; she's not yet ready to take them apart.

**Moving Ahead**    Ask your child. "Is *liz* part of *Elizabeth*?" "Is *ba* part of *banana*?" "Is *air* part of *airplane*?" If your child isn't sure, say the word slowly: *Elizabeth*. Ask her to raise a finger when she hears the syllable *liz*. When you start this activity, include only syllables that *are* part of the word. Later, give syllables that aren't part of the word: "Is *bat* part of *Elizabeth*?"

**Helpful Hint**    Don't use pencil and paper to explain syllables. What seems logical to an adult—reading or writing words syllable by syllable—will confuse your child. Let her focus on her hearing. On her own, your child will extend the concept to written words as she grows accustomed to reading and writing.

# 53 Chip In for Syllables

**H**elps develop: an ear for syllables

*Syllabication is a hard word to say, but your child will get the idea quickly.*

**Before You Begin**
Talk to your child about the way words sound. Some are short: *cat, ball, sun*. Some are longer: *umbrella, pony, monkey*.

The idea of this game is that each syllable of a word is worth something. It's easily played in an outdoor area where there are acorns or seeds available, and when your child is already playing with them.

**You'll Need**
a supply of small objects such as acorns, poker chips, pennies; a surface for lining up your small objects

**What to Do**
1 Divide a pile of acorns (or other small objects) into equal halves. Give your child half, and take half yourself.

2 Talk to your child about syllables, the sounds that fit together to make words. Say a couple of words and encourage your child to clap out the syllables with you. Here are some one-clap words: *tree, dog, friend*. Here are some two-clap words: *acorn, walnut, branches*. Here are some three-clap words: *halibut, underwear, octopus*.

3 Ask your child to give you a word. Tell him that for each syllable, you'll give him one of your acorns.

4 Have your child keep giving you words until he's earned all your acorns.

**Follow-up Activity**
Earn your acorns back. Give your child words. Let him figure out how many acorns to give you for each word.

**What's Happening**   *Young children can hear syllables but may need help identifying them as such. It may take plenty of experience to really get the concept—and our language can be very confusing to listen to. If necessary, have your child win all your acorns away from you with one-syllable words. Move on to two-syllable words gradually.*

**Moving Ahead**   Instead of using objects (acorns), make marks on paper. When a word has three syllables, for example, write three marks. This is one way of moving your child toward an understanding of how spoken words are written down on paper.

**Helpful Hint**   Make a habit of assessing words according to their worth in acorns: "Hey! I just heard you say a four-acorn word!"

# 54 Asking and Telling

**H**elps develop: an ear for the intonation of questions, exclamations, and declarative (telling) sentences

*I was pouring my dramatic heart and soul into reading a story when I realized the five-year-old's attention was on the type on the page. "There's another squiggly one!" she said, pointing to a question mark. "It's a questioner," explained her six-year-old sister. "It lets you ask questions." "Listen," I said, with a gleam in my eye, "See if you can hear the questions in this story."*

**Before You Begin**  Say to your child, "Listen, I'm going to say 'Little Jack Horner' as if it were all questions." Then do so. Silly, isn't it? At first, make this a silly dramatic game. Next, say the rhyme as if you were a reporter giving the six o'clock news. Then say it with exclamation points at the end of each line. Get your child in on the act with another rhyme or the same one said in a different way. Follow up with this activity, which helps your child differentiate between questions, exclamations, and declarative sentences.

**You'll Need**  a dramatic voice; nursery rhymes or other familiar lines

**What to Do**  
1 Say a simple sentence aloud: "The cat sat on the mat."

2 Ask your child, "Is that an asking or a telling sentence?" Help her decide.

3 Create a symbol for each kind of sentence. Your child might shrug dramatically for an asking sentence; point a finger at you for a telling sentence; jump and down for an exclamatory sentence; shake a finger for a command.

4 Take turns saying short sentences and responding with your symbol. Here are some examples to get you started.

- There's a bat in the attic!
- Do worms bite?
- Get me out of here!
- That story gives me the creeps!

- My book has four chapters.
- I'm so proud of you!
- I'm scratching mosquito bites.
- I'll have a peanut butter sandwich, please!

**Follow-up Activity**

Encourage your child to listen to the way people say sentences, and words within sentences. How can you tell when something's a question, a command, an exclamation, or a statement? One mother I know helped tune her children's ears to speech inflection by teasingly revoicing their questions: "What's for dinner, Mom?" became "What's for dinner? Mom?" "Who's at the door, Kim?" became "Who's at the door? Kim?" The kids got a giggle out of it, and learned some of the nuances of inflection—an important precursor to using punctuation and sentence construction clearly.

**What's Happening**

*Once again, you're helping your child make sense of the world. If you can name a thing, it's yours, even if it's a punctuation mark or a kind of sentence. For some children, punctuation marks are the first things that leap out from the page. Sure, children can identify letters, but letters alone don't help them make meaning of the page. Punctuation marks are necessary, too. "Hey!" says the child. "Someone in this story is talking . . . asking a question . . . getting excited . . . bossing someone around. Tell me what they're saying!" And you do, with intonation that lets them know: "You spotted a question, and here it is." This activity allows your child to represent physically the intonation she already understands by listening, and then, in the Moving Ahead activity, to represent it graphically.*

**Moving Ahead**

Make cards for your child: one question mark, one exclamation point, one period. Do the activity as described, but instead of using physical symbols, have your child hold up the appropriate punctuation mark symbol.

**Helpful Hint**

If your child wants to read a chapter for the punctuation marks alone, so be it. Let her spot the question marks, and read her the questions that precede them.

# 55 **Body English**

*This activity is a play on comedian and musician
Victor Borge's routine about oral punctuation,
in which he uses gestures and sounds to "read aloud"
punctuation with hilarious results.*

**H**elps develop:
*punctuation,
intonation, listening,
speaking, dramatic play*

**Before You Begin**    Play this game with a child who already knows that writing has punctuation marks in it to give the reader information but that spoken language has no punctuation marks. Ask your child, "How can you tell when I'm asking you a question, giving a command, or telling you something someone said?" Possible answers include: tone of voice, context, direct reference such as "So I asked . . ." or "He was yelling . . ."

**You'll Need**    you and your child

**What to Do**    **1** Tell your child a story using physical symbols as punctuation marks: a question mark drawn in the air after a question, an exclamation point drawn in the air after a command or emotional statement, and quotation marks indicated by both hands raised, the first and second fingers pointing downwards, before and after a quotation.

   Here's an example of a good story to tell using physical punctuation symbols:

> Knock, knock.
> Someone was knocking at the little pig's door.
> Who could it be?
> "Who is it?" called the little pig.
> "Little pig, little pig, let me come in!" growled the wolf.
> "Not by the hair of my chinny-chin-chin!" answered the pig.
> "Then I'll huff, and I'll puff, and I'll blow your house in!"

**2** Have your child tell you a story in the same manner.

**CLOSE TO HOME**

**Follow-up Activity**  Add sound effects to your punctuation in the classic Victor Borge style. An exclamation point, for example, becomes a whistling sound on the downstroke, and a popping sound for the dot.

*What's Happening*  You're making visual something that's usually invisible in spoken language. You're making physical something that's usually graphic. And you're helping your child make one giant leap toward using punctuation purposefully in his own writing.

**Moving Ahead**  Read a simple play with your child. Show him how the playwright uses stage directions as well as italicized words for emphasis and punctuation. Note that quotation marks are not used in plays, where spoken words are the main thing. Note how actions are suggested in stage directions.

**Helpful Hint**  Your child is never too young for Victor Borge. Show him a videotape of Borge doing his oral punctuation and other routines. Your child will be pleased to have learned to use a comic routine in his own way. Borge uses lots of language gags in his routines. Help your child spot them.

# 56 **Put a Cap on It**

*Big A, little a, bouncing B . . .*
*Cat's in the cupboard, and she can't see.*

**Before You Begin**  Copy the rhyme above onto a sheet of paper or poster board. Read it with your child, pointing out the uppercase (capital) and lowercase *As*, *Bs*, and *Cs*. Tell your child that every letter has at least two forms.

**You'll Need**  pencil; paper or poster board; index cards; magazines and newspapers; typewriter or word processor (optional)

**What to Do**

**1** Draw a line to divide each of 26 index cards in half.

**2** On one half of each card, draw an uppercase letter. On the other half, draw the lowercase version of the letter. Do this for all 26 letters of the alphabet. Show the cards to your child.

**3** Talk with her about the different forms uppercase and lowercase letters take: for example, *G* and *g* are completely different, but *C* and *c* vary only in size.

**4** Cut the cards in half to separate the uppercase and lowercase forms.

**5** Mix up the cards. Place them in a pile face down.

**6** With your child, take turns drawing cards from the pile. Place the cards you draw face up in front of you and have your child do the same. Help your child try to make matches with new cards drawn from the pile.

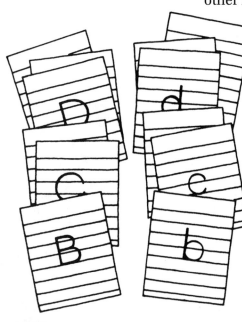

**Follow-up Activity**    Make another set of cards from printed letters. Use a variety of fonts from your computer, or cut capital and lowercase letters from magazines and newspapers. Invite your child to match these cards with their capital and lowercase partners, and with the corresponding handwritten cards.

**What's Happening**    *Many children come to school already knowing how to write their names, but the use of uppercase and lowercase letters varies. Some write in all capitals. Many write the first letter of their name as a capital, but don't recognize the lowercase form of that letter as part of the name—to them, it just isn't. When children start reading, they see uppercase and lowercase letters in rich—and confusing—profusion. Not only do letters have uppercase and lowercase versions, they may have different forms of each. Think of the different ways of writing lowercase* a, *for example. It helps children to expose them to all the different forms letters take and to talk about them. Talk about the family of* A *if you wish, including the print and script forms, the uppercase and lowercase forms. Once again, you're helping your child make meaning of what can otherwise be a wash of seemingly unrelated symbols.*

**Moving Ahead**    Use the index cards as a guide as your child searches for letters on a page of a newspaper or magazine. Choose one letter at a time and ask your child to circle all the examples of this letter she can find.

**Helpful Hint**    Once your child knows the uses of uppercase and lowercase letters, type or write a passage using only lowercase letters. Ask your child to edit your work, circling letters that should be capitals. Ask your editor to explain why a capital letter is needed in each place she suggests.

# 57 The Big Squeeze

*Helps develop: understanding of the purpose, punctuation, and spelling of contractions*

*Where'd the o go? It's out of place.*
*It rolled away to save some space.*

**Before You Begin**  Talk to your child about shortcuts. Point out what she's doing when she walks across the corner of a lawn to get to the path, or jumps from the second step rather than walking to the bottom. Tell her that people take shortcuts when they talk and write too.

**You'll Need**  paper and pencil

**What to Do**  
**1** Talk with your child about how people shorten words when they talk fast. Demonstrate with these two sentences: "I cannot wait until it is my birthday, but I have got to." versus "I can't wait 'til it's my birthday, but I've got to."

**2** Talk about which parts of the first sentence above were dropped out to make the sentence go more quickly. Tell your child that writers do this, too, and that people over time have figured out ways to write words more quickly.

**3** Demonstrate this by writing words on a sheet of paper, one pair per sheet: *does not, cannot, I have.*

**4** Now show your child how the words are shortened by tearing your paper into strips of letters. Throw out the letters that disappear in the contraction form. Put the strips together to show how the contraction looks.

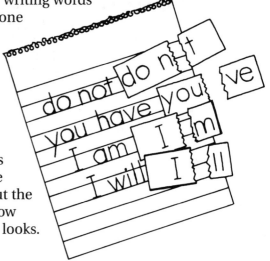

**Follow-up Activity**   Invite your child to make a contraction out of a pair of words by tearing the letters out as you did in the steps above. Encourage her to *hear* what's missing and then to figure out which letters were removed to correspond with the sounds.

**Moving Ahead**   Give your child a slip of paper with an apostrophe on it to slip into the place where the letter or letters are missing in a contraction. Talk about this punctuation mark, which stands for something missing. Talk about its use in place of letters dropped from words like *'til* and *'em*. Signs on stores can be especially useful for this game.

**Helpful Hint**   Here are some more examples of contractions and spellings with letters dropped.

| | |
|---|---|
| haven't | *have not* |
| won't | *will not* |
| didn't | *did not* |
| aren't | *are not* |
| you've | *you have* |
| they'd | *they would* |
| she'll | *she will* |
| I'm | *I am* |
| fishin' | *fishing* |
| li'l | *little* |
| rock 'n' roll | *rock and roll* |
| 'twas | *it was* |

# 58 **Color Game**

*elps develop:* **H** *vocabulary, following directions, giving directions, reading sight words*

*Put the red crayon* on *the black paper.*
*Hold the green crayon* above *the yellow paper.*

**Before You Begin**  Have your child make this game with you, and then play it together.

**You'll Need**  a basic box of 8 crayons; sheets of construction paper in 8 colors; 24 small pieces of paper; 3 bags or boxes

**What to Do**  
**1** Divide the small pieces of paper into three piles of 8 pieces.

**2** Take the first pile of eight. Using a crayon, write the name of the crayon's color on one of the pieces of paper. (For example, write "red" with the red crayon.) Repeat with the remaining crayons and pieces of paper. You'll end up with eight pieces of paper with eight different color names, written in their colors. Put the pile in a bag or box and label it "crayons."

**3** Take the second pile of eight. With any color crayon, write the names of the colors of construction paper, one color name to each piece of paper, or cut off a little square of the construction paper, glue it on your small paper, and label it. Put this pile in a second bag or box and label this one "construction paper."

**4** Take the third pile of eight. Again with any color crayon, write the following words, one to each piece of paper: *on, under, beside, above, across, between, left, right.* Put this pile in a third bag or box, and label it "words."

**5** Line up the three bags and put the crayons and the construction paper next to the bags.

**6** Take turns pulling a paper from the "crayon" bag. Pick up the crayon it matches.

**7** Take a paper from the "construction paper" bag. This indicates which sheet of colored paper to take.

**8** Take a paper from the "word" bag. This indicates what to do with the crayon in relation to the colored paper: Place the crayon *on, under, beside,* or *above* the paper, as directed by the word paper.

**Follow-up Activity** Substitute different objects (such as toy cars or wooden blocks) for the crayons and construction paper. Place them in paper bags. Have your child draw one object from each bag and then draw one word from the word bag. Invite your child to use the word card to place the objects in relation to each other. Then ask your child to describe the position of the objects, using their names and the word that shows their relationship: for example, "The car is under the block."

**What's Happening** This game causes players to make associations between basic words, objects, and actions. By making the game with you, your child gains experience with the words even before using them.

**Moving Ahead** Eliminate the use of colors and just write the words that stand for the colors.

**Helpful Hint** Help your child to further discriminate between colors and to name them by allowing him to explore boxes of threads, crayons, paint sample charts, and cloth samples.

# 59 Singular and Plural

---

**H**elps develop:
concepts of
singular and plural,
understanding of how
nouns are made plural,
vocabulary

*"OOH! I love those meeces to pieces!"*
*The cartoon cat who uttered those immortal words*
*hadn't mastered his plural vocabulary yet—but he knew*
*the difference between one and many.*

---

**Before You Begin**   Go through a magazine with your child. Ask her to select ten pictures of things. Tear or cut them out and put them in a pile. Make sure she has a good representation of single objects and objects in groups of two or more. Pick a few yourself to make sure.

**You'll Need**   old magazines; a list of words like the one on the next page in Helpful Hint

**What to Do**   **1** Look at the pictures with your child. One of you chooses a picture and names the object or objects pictured, using a noun: *bear, cups, feet, bell.*

**2** The other person responds by holding up one finger for a singular noun, all ten fingers for a plural noun. If your child holds up the same number of fingers as there are things in the picture, say, three, say, "Is it one, or more than one?"

**Follow-up Activity**   When you've gone through all your pictures, switch to a list of written words. Use the words shown in the Helpful Hint below, or create your own list of words that might be more meaningful to your child. Ask your child to raise fingers again. Emphasize that she use either one finger or all.

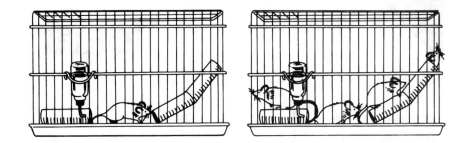

You're focusing on nouns, first with pictures, then through words alone, and you're zeroing in on whether each is singular or plural. As your child gains practice, she will begin to classify the nouns, realizing that some mean one and some mean more than one. She'll make generalizations about how plural nouns are formed. When your child realizes (and this may happen long before you do this activity) that the addition of an s to a noun makes it plural, she may say mouses (probably not meeces) instead of mice. There's no need to correct her; she's just experimenting. Soon enough she'll realize that in English there are exceptions to many rules.

**Moving Ahead**    Work with your child to create collages of "one" and "lots," illustrating these concepts with photographs and labeling them with invented writing.

**Helpful Hint**    Here's that list of singular and plural words you can use:

| dog | mice | place | kitten |
|-----|------|-------|--------|
| houses | kisses | swings | cars |
| lion | desk | rubber bands | glass |
| lionesses | pencil | toothbrushes | screen |
| alligators | hat | | |

# 60 **Board Games**

Here's a new use for that board game
that you and your child
are a little bored with.

**H**elps develop: *letter/sound relationships, spelling, vocabulary*

**Before You Begin**  Gather some movable letters and put them in a bag where they can't be seen. Set up an old board game as usual.

**You'll Need**  a board game that involves progressing toward a goal, such as Candyland, checkers, or Chutes and Ladders; movable letters; bag

**What to Do**  1 Play your board game as usual. For example, if you use checkers, take turns moving forward as usual. But before each player takes a turn, he must reach into the bag and take a movable letter.

2 The player must then say the sound (or one of the sounds) this letter makes, and give an example of how that letter is used in a word. For example, your child picks *S*. She must make the *S* sound and give a word that has *S* in it: *snake*. Then she can take her turn. Write down the words players give to avoid repetition and to demonstrate spelling.

3 Each player must check the other players' answers to verify that the word uses the same sound as the movable letter. If it doesn't, the player loses that turn.

4 Continue to play the board game by the usual rules until someone wins or goes out.

**Follow-up Activity**  Alter the game's rules to suit you. If you and your child want a game that's noncompetitive, play it that way. Play Candyland until everyone gets to the candy castle. Eliminate steps that send a player back to Start, or play as a team, helping each other get to the goal.

Y*ou're not just giving your child more practice in sounds and spellings, you're helping him learn something important about games—that they exist for fun and pleasure, work flexibly, and can be changed and adapted to suit your needs.*

**Moving Ahead**     Create your own board game with your child, using poster board to create a game board. Let your child draw a large maze or path on the board. Use round or square stickers to create spots to land on. Use extra dice from another game. Put something exciting on the board as a goal, as well as pitfalls along the way. Use the game to practice language skills as you did in the activity above.

**Helpful Hint**     Any game at all can be used to reinforce whatever language skill you want to practice with your child. The language skills given here are just examples. Pick your own.

- Twister—Let each color stand for a letter. If the spinner points to red, each player must give a word starting with that letter in order to win the place for his foot or hand.

- Tag—Chase your child around. When you're about to tag him, he can save himself by sitting down quickly and calling out a word that has a *K* sound in it.

- Tic-Tac-Toe—Draw the 9-square grid. Instead of using *X*s and *O*s, use *L*s and *P*s. To gain a square for your letter, first give a word that ends with that letter.

# Activities Index

**About the Authors**

**Marlene Barron** is an internationally known educator and authority on the educational and developmental needs of preschool and elementary school children. She holds a Ph.D. in Early Childhood and Elementary Education. Her focus is early literacy development. She is Head of West Side Montessori School in New York City and a professor at New York University. Dr. Barron gives frequent lectures and workshops on early childhood education around the country and also publishes articles in professional journals. She is the author of *I Learn to Read and Write the Way I Learn to Talk: A Very First Book About Whole Language.*

**Karen Romano Young** is a writer specializing in educational materials for children, teachers, and parents. Formerly an editor at Scholastic, she has written for The National Geographic Society and Children's Television Workshop. Her work has appeared in books, magazines, and other media. Ms. Young holds a B.S. in elementary education and is the mother of three children.